D0048197

Letters to Churches... Then and Now

BIBLE STUDY GUIDE

From the Bible-teaching ministry of

Charles R. Swindoll

INSIGHT FOR LIVING

Charles R. Swindoll is a graduate of Dallas Theological Seminary and has served in pastorates for more than twenty-three years, including churches in Texas, New England, and California. Since 1971 he has served as senior pastor of the First Evangelical Free Church of Fullerton, California. Chuck's radio program, "Insight for Living," began in 1979. In addition to his church and radio ministries, Chuck has authored twenty-one books and numerous booklets on a variety of subjects.

Based on the outlines of Chuck's sermons, the study guide text is coauthored by Bill Watkins, a graduate of California State University at Fresno and Dallas Theological Seminary. The Living Insights are written by Bill Butterworth, a graduate of Florida Bible College, Dallas Theological Seminary, and Florida Atlantic University. He is currently the director of counseling ministries.

Editor in Chief:	Cynthia Swindoll
Coauthor of Text:	Bill Watkins
Author of Living Insights:	Bill Butterworth
Editorial Assistant:	Julie Martin
Copy Manager:	Jac La Tour
Senior Copy Assistant:	Jane Gillis
Copy Assistant:	Glenda Schlahta
Director, Communications Division:	Carla Beck
Project Manager:	Nina Paris
Art Director:	Becky Englund
Production Artist:	Donna Mayo
Typographer:	Bob Haskins
Cover Photograph:	G. Robert Nease
Print Production Manager:	Deedee Snyder
Printer:	Frye and Smith

Unless otherwise identified, all Scripture references are from the New American Standard Bible, © The Lockman Foundation 1960, 1962, 1963, 1968, 1971, 1972, 1973, 1975, 1977. Used by permission.

ISBN 0-8499-8290-1

Ordering Information

An album that contains ten messages on five cassettes and corresponds to this study guide may be purchased through Insight for Living, Post Office Box 4444, Fullerton, California 92634. For ordering information and a current catalog, please write our office or call (714) 870-9161.

Canadian residents may obtain a catalog and ordering information through Insight for Living Ministries, Post Office Box 2510, Vancouver, British Columbia, Canada V6B 3W7, (604) 272-5811. Overseas residents should direct their correspondence to our Fullerton office.

If you wish to order by Visa or MasterCard, you are welcome to use our toll-free number, (800) 772-8888, Monday through Friday between the hours of 8:30 A.M. and 4:00 P.M., Pacific time. This number may be used anywhere in the continental United States excluding Alaska, California, and Hawaii. Orders from those areas can be made by calling our general office number, (714) 870-9161.

Table of Contents

Letters to Churches . . .
Then and Now

Many Christians are surprised that some of the most practical truths in the New Testament are tucked away in the book of Revelation. This grand, final book of the Bible is more than a prophetic panorama of God's world program.

In the second and third chapters of Revelation, there appears a stack of letters—seven in all—addressed to first-century churches much like ones across our land. The relevance of these letters is nothing short of amazing. You will think the Spirit of God has been looking in on your church!

As we examine each letter and apply its contents to twentieth-century Christianity, let's be sensitive to the voice of God. Let's welcome His counsel, accept His evaluation, heed His warnings, and respond to His reproofs. In the final analysis, this is the only way we can lift the print off the pages of these inspired letters and incarnate the truth.

Chuck Swindoll

Chuck Swindoll

Putting Truth into Action

Knowledge apart from application falls short of God's desire for His children. Knowledge must result in change and growth. Consequently, we have constructed this Bible study guide with these purposes in mind: (1) to stimulate discovery, (2) to increase understanding, and (3) to encourage application.

At the end of each lesson is a section called 🐎 **Living Insights.** There you'll be given assistance in further Bible study, thoughtful interaction, and personal appropriation. This is the place where the lesson is fitted with shoe leather for your walk through the varied experiences of life.

It's our hope that you'll discover numerous ways to use this tool. Some useful avenues we would suggest are personal meditation, joint discovery, and discussion with your spouse, family, work associates, friends, or neighbors. The study guide is also practical for church classes and, of course, as a study aid for the "Insight for Living" radio broadcast.

In order to derive the greatest benefit from this process, we suggest that you record your responses to the lessons in a notebook where writing space is plentiful. In view of the kinds of questions asked, your notebook may become a journal filled with your many discoveries and commitments. We anticipate that you will find yourself returning to it periodically for review and encouragement.

Bill Watkins
Coauthor of Text

Bill Butterworth
Author of Living Insights

Letters to Churches...
Then and Now

Royal Mail in the Postman's Bag
Revelation 1

Have you ever received a letter from a close friend in which love was expressed . . . along with carefully worded criticism—a letter of commendation mixed with some painfully frank suggestions for improvement? What if a letter like that came from your fiancé? What would your response be? Would you be angry and bitter . . . or repentant and accepting? Imagine that letter coming from the Bridegroom of the Church—Jesus Christ—the One who loves you most. Would you accept what He had to say about your relationship to Him? Would you change aspects of your life if He asked you to? Would you do all you could to present yourself as a pure bride to Him, your Groom? You'll get a chance to answer these questions in our study of Christ's letters preserved in The Revelation to John. Although this divine correspondence was originally addressed to seven churches in Asia Minor, it has timeless messages that each of us in the Church—the Bride of Christ—need to hear and heed. Are you ready to read your royal love mail, the letters from your kingly Groom? Tear open the envelope and unfold the letter of Revelation. Then ask God to open your heart to the words that await your personal response.

I. Common Reactions
Some people hold strong opinions about Revelation. Before we look at Christ's letters, let's examine three common points of view.

A. "It's confusing." Some people view Revelation as if it were written in a secret code—one that only God can crack. The book's array of strange creatures and symbolic language leaves these individuals bewildered. Unfortunately, much of this confusion is generated by ministers whose sermons on Revelation offer highly imaginative and sometimes contradictory interpretations. The book itself, however, usually gives the key to understanding its metaphors and visions to the extent that God desires.

B. "It's the meat of God's Word." Other people are extremists, who think of Revelation as the most important book in the Bible. To them, life revolves around understanding, proclaiming, discussing, and anticipating end-time events. They often carry

1

detailed, multi-colored charts that plot every major and minor future happening predicted in Scripture. Every number and every detail in every vision has profound significance to them. Their curiosity is commendable, but their extremism is harmful. An overemphasis on prophecy leads individuals to live unbalanced lives that frequently discredit Christianity in the eyes of the world. We need to guard against this kind of attitude.

C. "It's irrelevant to everyday life." This response is the most disturbing of the three. Those who give it see Revelation as a book about the there and then with no here-and-now application. Revelation, to them, unveils a futuristic scenario that is more appropriate for an episode of "The Twilight Zone" than for the common man's workaday world. As we'll see, their opinion could not be further from the truth. The heavenly visions of Revelation have great earthly value. Their purpose is not to confuse, fascinate, or entertain us but to motivate us to live Christianly in an alien, hostile world. How much more relevant could Revelation be?

II. Basic Observations

Up-to-date letters for up-to-date churches . . . and members! Let's open this ancient correspondence and learn what it has to tell us. The first nine verses of chapter 1 will give us some clues to understanding the rest.

A. Its title and purpose. The opening five words, "The Revelation of Jesus Christ," give the title and purpose of the book. The rest of verse 1 indicates that Revelation is a disclosure of events yet to come—happenings in which Jesus Christ is the central figure. It also conveys that God the Father gave the revelation to His Son, Christ, so that He would in turn "show [it] to His bond-servants." In short, Jesus is both the revealer and the revelation of this book. He is the One it came through, and He is its central character. Looking at the book as a whole, we can see that "[its] main purpose is to reveal the person of the Lord Jesus Christ as the Redeemer of the world and as the conqueror of evil, and to present in symbolic form the program by which He will carry out His work."[1]

B. Its recipient. Christ communicated His revelation through "His angel to His bond-servant John" (v. 1b). The identity of this particular angel is uncertain, but the identity of the human recipient is clear. He was the Apostle John, the one who wrote

---

1. Merrill C. Tenney, "Revelation," in *Master Study Bible: New American Standard* (Nashville, Tenn.: Holman Bible Publishers, 1981), p. 1290.

the Fourth Gospel and the three epistles that bear his name.[2] This man was with Jesus during His earthly ministry; he watched Christ die, was asked to care for His mother, encountered Him after His resurrection, and witnessed His ascension into heaven (John 19:26–30, 21:4–7). John was the disciple Jesus particularly loved and trusted (John 13:23, 19:26–27, 20:2).[3]

C. Its promise. John assures us that those who hear, read, and obey the contents of Revelation will be blessed (Rev. 1:3). This promise demonstrates that the book was given to encourage us toward godly living, not merely to inform us about future happenings.

D. Its date and geographic origin. The contents of Revelation were unveiled to John while he was on Patmos (v. 9)—an island in the Aegean Sea that lies about thirty-seven miles west of Miletus.[4] According to early church tradition, the Roman authorities had exiled the Apostle John to this ancient Alcatraz because he refused to recant his faith in Christ. Banishment was apparently Emperor Domitian's favorite way of purging Christians from the Roman Empire. Unlike his predecessor Nero, whose focus was on slaughtering Roman believers, Domitian undertook an unprecedented empire-wide persecution of Christians. John's strong stand for Jesus caused him to become one of Domitian's victims (v. 9).[5]

III. Initial Communication

In the last eleven verses of Revelation 1, we are allowed a glimpse of John's island encounter with the risen Lord.

A. When did it occur? John says the vision began while he "was in the Spirit on the Lord's day" (v. 10a). Although there is some

---

2. Donald Guthrie provides several reasons for accepting the Apostle John as Revelation's human writer in his *New Testament Introduction*, 3d ed. (Downers Grove, Ill.: InterVarsity Press, 1970), pp. 934–49.

3. See Guthrie, *New Testament Introduction*, pp. 245–46.

4. Of this island, expositor Alan Johnson writes: "Consisting mainly of volcanic hills and rocky ground, Patmos is about ten miles long and six miles wide at the north end. It was an island used for Roman penal purposes. [Roman historian] Tacitus refers to the use of such small islands for political banishment (*Annals* 3.68; 4.30; 15.71). [The church historian] Eusebius mentions that John was banished to the island by the emperor Domitian in A.D. 95 and released eighteen months later by [Domitian's successor] Nerva (*Ecclesiastical History* 3.20. 8–9)." "Revelation," in *The Expositor's Bible Commentary* (Grand Rapids, Mich.: Regency Reference Library, Zondervan Publishing House, 1981), p. 424.

5. One source that supports a mid-90s A.D. composition date for Revelation is *The Book of Revelation*, by Robert H. Mounce (Grand Rapids, Mich.: William B. Eerdmans Publishing Co., 1977), pp. 31–36. A scholar who represents the growing number of commentators adopting a 70 or pre-70 A.D. date of composition is John A. T. Robinson. See his book *Redating the New Testament* (Philadelphia, Penn.: The Westminster Press, 1976), chap. 8.

question as to what he meant by "the Lord's day," it has commonly been interpreted as a reference to Sunday, the Christian Sabbath. On this day of lonely worship, John was mentally transported from his earthly setting of tribulation and despair to a heavenly scene of triumph and hope. For us as well, Christ provides times of reprieve when our worries reach their peak and our future seems foreboding.

B. What did John hear? "A loud voice like the sound of a trumpet" (v. 10b) blasting out two commands: first, to record in a scroll what he saw (v. 11a) and second, to send his account to seven specific churches (v. 11b). All in western Asia Minor, these were the assemblies at Ephesus, Smyrna, Pergamum, Thyatira, Sardis, Philadelphia, and Laodicea. The map below shows the exact location of these cities, the Roman road that connected them, and their proximity to Patmos.[6]

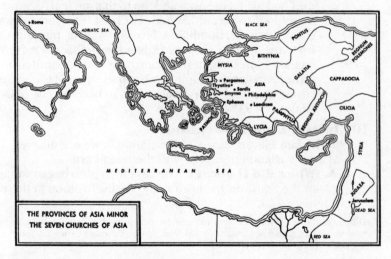

THE PROVINCES OF ASIA MINOR
THE SEVEN CHURCHES OF ASIA

C. Why were these churches singled out? Many answers have been given to this question. A popular one is that these seven churches represent seven major periods in church history. Advocates of this view sometimes interpret the Ephesian church as symbolic of the apostolic era, the Smyrnian church as representative of the post-apostolic era, and so on to the Laodicean church as standing for the Church today. There are two major problems with this interpretive approach: (1) it is so subjective

---

6. Permission to use this map was graciously provided by William B. Eerdmans Publishing Company and also appears in a book by Merrill C. Tenney titled *Interpreting Revelation* (Grand Rapids, Mich.: William B. Eerdmans Publishing Co., 1957), p. 53.

that even its proponents disagree on which church represents which historical period, and (2) it ignores or discounts the fact that these seven churches actually existed in the first century and had the needs and problems that Revelation says they had. In other words, the heavenly voice had specific messages designed to address the real needs of specific churches. However, since the difficulties these congregations faced have been encountered by other congregations throughout history, even to our own day, the messages meant for the original seven churches are just as relevant now as they were then.

D. Who was the source of the trumpetlike voice? When John turned to find out, he saw a figure impossible to describe except by means of analogy:

> And having turned I saw seven golden lampstands; and in the middle of the lampstands one like a son of man, clothed in a robe reaching to the feet, and girded across His breast with a golden girdle. And His head and His hair were white like white wool, like snow; and His eyes were like a flame of fire; and His feet were like burnished bronze, when it has been caused to glow in a furnace, and His voice was like the sound of many waters. And in His right hand He held seven stars; and out of His mouth came a sharp two-edged sword; and His face was like the sun shining in its strength. (Rev. 1:12b–16)

"When I saw Him," John adds, "I fell at His feet as a dead man" (v. 17a). Who was this awesome person? He was " 'the first and the last, and the living One' " (vv. 17b–18a). He was the person who was once dead but is now " 'alive forevermore' "—the One who holds " 'the keys of death and of Hades' " (v. 18). This individual was none other than the resurrected, glorified Christ. Only God can be " 'the Alpha and the Omega, . . . who is and who was and who is to come, the Almighty' " (v. 8). And only the Son of God came to earth to die as payment for human sin and rose from the grave in triumph over death (compare v. 5). At the sight of His radiant holiness, John fell to the ground, just as Saul did on the road to Damascus (Acts 9:3–4). One day, every human being will see the risen Lord face-to-face. For some, it will mark the beginning of everlasting celebration (1 John 3:2, Rev. 21:1–22:5). For others, their encounter will be the beginning of everlasting despair (2 Thess. 1:7–9; Rev. 20:11–15, 21:8). What will this day mean for you?

E. What do the stars and lampstands symbolize? According to Revelation 1:20, the seven lampstands are the seven churches specified in verse 11. The seven stars represent " 'the angels of the seven churches.' " But who were the angels? Were they heavenly guardians of the seven churches? Perhaps, but it seems strange that Christ would address His correspondence to angelic beings when the content of His letters obviously concerned the churches themselves. Questions such as this have led many commentators to identify the angels as human messengers. The Greek word for *angel* is sometimes used in Scripture to refer to human messengers (Matt. 11:7–10, Luke 9:52). In Revelation 1–3, the term probably refers to the pastors or main teachers of the seven churches, or to prophets through whom the messages of the letters were to be delivered to the local congregations.[7] At any rate, there is no question that Christ had picked the Apostle John to be the postman for His royal mail. And the mail John was to deliver was originally for seven first-century churches to hear and heed.

IV. Personal Application

Moving from the first century to our own, we can recognize at least three truths from Revelation 1 that have practical significance for our own churches and lives today.

A. Christ still stands at the center of His Church. As He told Simon Peter, "I will build my church; and the gates of Hades *shall not* overpower it" (Matt. 16:18b, emphasis added). Here, the Lord Jesus underscores the fact that He is the hub of His Church. He is responsible. It is His obligation to sustain the life of His Bride. Unfaithful though she may be, weak though she may become, He is at the center. He is there. And He wants to be at the center not only of His Church but of each believer's life as well. Do the spokes of your life radiate from the strong hub of Jesus? Or does your life seem to be lacking that centricity to give balance and stability?

B. God still speaks through the authority of His Word. Notice the description of God's Word in Hebrews 4:12: "For the Word of God is living and active and sharper than any two-edged sword, and piercing as far as the division of soul and spirit, of both joints and marrow, and able to judge the thoughts and intentions of the heart." His Word hasn't lost its potency. It is still a two-edged sword . . . the only accurate judge of the heart's motives. It is still timely . . . still authoritative . . . still reliable . . . still alive. How open are you to surgery by the blade of God's Word? Are you willing to submit to its sharp edge, or are you rushing around looking for second opinions in a frenzy of denial?

---

7. See John Walvoord's *The Revelation of Jesus Christ* (Chicago, Ill.: Moody Press, 1966), p. 53.

Surgery is sometimes a scary thing, but refusing to operate on the malignant tumor of sin is a mistake of terminal proportions.

C. **Unfortunately, few still fall at the Lord's feet in praise and humility.** In our high-tech world, where the song on everyone's lips is "Sweet Self-Sufficiency," few pause to bow before the Lord and give Him the honor He deserves. Like the Pharisee who came to pray at the temple, too often we remind God how righteous we are, how much we give, how religious we've become (Luke 18:9–12). We seem to forget that God strengthens us most when our own hearts are weak and worn. Only when we come before Him prostrate and broken do we see ourselves in the right light—as people desperately dependent on God, like the tax-gatherer who also came to the temple to pray and said simply: "God, be merciful to me, a sinner!" Only when we humble ourselves at His feet do we gain His favor (vv. 18:12–13). It's easier to unload our burdens when we bend our backs and fall at His feet. Have you been carrying the load of the Christian life on self-sufficient shoulders, or are you coming to Him to unload that burden? Remember His words: "Come to Me all who are weary and heavy laden, and I will give you rest" (Matt. 11:28).

 Living Insights

Study One ▬▬▬▬▬▬▬▬▬▬▬▬▬▬▬▬▬▬▬▬▬▬▬▬▬▬▬▬▬▬▬

Let's look into the messages to the seven churches in Revelation 2–3. If you've read this passage before, try to block out previous thoughts and take a fresh approach. As you read about the churches, jot down initial impressions about each one. Copy this chart into your notebook and record your comments so that you can look back on them. It will be interesting to compare your first thoughts to the things you learn as you continue your study of the letters to the churches.

Churches	Verses	Initial Impressions
Ephesus	2:1–7	
Smyrna	2:8–11	
Pergamum	2:12–17	
Thyatira	2:18–29	
Sardis	3:1–6	
Philadelphia	3:7–13	
Laodicea	3:14–19	

Continued on next page

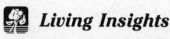 *Living Insights*

As you read over these letters to churches, did you find them applicable to your own life? Did certain messages hit closer to home than others? Did some remind you of past times in your life?

- Skim over Revelation 2–3. Copy this chart into your notebook and in the right-hand column, write appropriate applications to your personal life. These may involve either present or past struggles. Don't force the text, but do look for truths that relate to you.

Churches	Verses	Appropriate Applications
Ephesus	2:1–7	
Smyrna	2:8–11	
Pergamum	2:12–17	
Thyatira	2:18–29	
Sardis	3:1–6	
Philadelphia	3:7–13	
Laodicea	3:14–19	

Everything but the One Thing
Revelation 2:1–7

Shattered windows, dried-out shingles, peeling paint, overgrown grass, untrimmed shrubs . . . all signs of a home that has lost its life. Perhaps such a place once rang with the laughter of a young married couple or sheltered a busy, growing, loving family. It may have provided comfort and fond memories for a nice elderly couple. But now it stands uninhabited . . . a discarded shell. What a sad picture! And yet, a house that has become lifeless is not as tragic as a church that has become loveless. Imagine a congregation with a vital commitment to Christ growing stagnant and indifferent. Perhaps it remains doctrinally orthodox, evangelistically active, and socially responsible, but its orthodoxy and activities are no longer maintained out of a deep devotion to the Lord. Do you attend a church like this? Has your fire for Christ died out? The believers in the church at Ephesus allowed their flame to grow cold, and Jesus confronted them about it in no uncertain terms. However, with characteristic kindness, He also provided them with a solution. If you or your church has lost the fire for Christ, you can find the fuel for rekindling it in His letter to Ephesus.

I. Background of the Ephesian Church

The church of Ephesus was probably founded by the Apostle Paul, Aquila, and Priscilla (Acts 18:18–19, 24–26; 19:1–10). Paul ministered there for more than two years (19:8–10) and later left Timothy in that city to carry on the already flourishing work (1 Tim. 1:3). Christian tradition has it that after Jesus' resurrection, the Apostle John brought Christ's mother Mary to Ephesus, where they took up residence during their remaining years (see John 19:27). Paul probably spent so much time ministering in Ephesus because of the city's strategic importance. It was known as the Supreme Metropolis of Asia. Along with Antioch on the Orontes River and Egypt's Alexandria, Ephesus was ranked as one of the top three cities of the eastern Mediterranean. Economically, the city thrived as a result of its prosperous sea trade, made possible by an inland harbor connected with the Cayster River.[1] Also, "Merchandise of every description from the East and West poured into its spacious warehouses stretching along the

---

1. "Land trade supplemented sea trade in augmenting the prosperity of the city. Besides easy access to the interior of Asia by interlacing highways and to the East by the great road running through Laodicea, Colossae, Apamaea, Pisidian Antioch, Tarsus and Syrian Antioch, Ephesus owned extensive districts in its environs, notably the coastal regions southward, including the cities of Phygela and Marathesium. The lower Cayster Valley, including the city of Larissa, also was a part of the large landed interests of the city that helped to swell its income and increase its reputation as a populous and opulent commercial center. . . . [Ephesus's] population has been estimated to have exceeded a quarter of a million." Merrill F. Unger, *Archaeology and the New Testament* (Grand Rapids, Mich.: Zondervan Publishing House, 1962), p. 250.

river and up the sides of Mount Coressos."[2] Ephesus was also significant politically. It was the home of the Roman governor and frequently the scene of important trials. Religiously, Ephesus was the hub of the worship of Artemis, or Diana.[3] It was in this economically wealthy, politically influential, and religiously corrupt city that a congregation of Christians met for worship, discipleship, and evangelism. And this was one of the churches that received a personal letter from Jesus Christ Himself.

II. Introduction to the First Letter

Revelation 2:1–7 records the letter originally sent to the Ephesian church. It was mailed " 'to the attention of the angel of the church' " (v. 1a)—probably the pastor or teaching elder. The author of the letter is Christ, who identifies Himself as " 'the One who holds the seven stars in His right hand, the One who walks among the seven golden lampstands' " (v. 1b). In our first lesson, we identified the stars as the churches' pastors and the lampstands as the churches themselves. Continuing this imagery, Jesus is saying that *He* is the protector, sustainer, and head of the churches. He is the One to whom both leaders and laypeople are ultimately accountable, as well as the One on whom they are always dependent. The symbolism of Christ walking among the lampstands indicates His continual presence. This thought is both reassuring and threatening. As Psalm 139 reveals, the Lord's presence means inescapable, penetrating knowledge. Everything is naked and exposed to His gaze (see Heb. 4:13).

> ### A Thought to Consider
> Do you live in the knowledge that Christ is always with you—reading your every thought, perceiving your every motive, hearing your every word, and watching your every action? Do you rely on Him, rest in Him, and respond to Him in obedience to His Word? Do you realize that one day you will have to answer to Him for the way you have lived (1 Cor. 3:10–15)? Consider these questions carefully; answer them honestly and make changes if necessary. This self-examination may be painful, but it will result in abundant blessing.

---

2. Unger, *Archaeology and the New Testament,* p. 250.

3. The temple, with its statue of the goddess Artemis, was considered one of the seven wonders of the ancient world. "Thousands of priests and priestesses were involved in [Artemis's] service. Many of the priestesses were dedicated to cult prostitution. . . . The temple also served as a great bank for kings and merchants, as well as an asylum for fleeing criminals." Alan F. Johnson, "Revelation," in *The Expositor's Bible Commentary* (Grand Rapids, Mich.: Regency Reference Library, Zondervan Publishing House, 1981), vol. 12, p. 433.

III. Analysis of the Ephesian Christians

As the letter continues, the Lord names three areas of strength and one area of weakness that characterized the believers in first-century Ephesus.

A. Commended strengths. Jesus recognized that the Ephesian Christians were *energetic* and *hard-working* (Rev. 2:2a). They lived in a city where paganism and immorality ran rampant. But instead of huddling in a corner and hiding from the spiritual war raging around them, they stepped into the fray and wielded the sword of the gospel bravely and consistently. Christ also observed the believers' *perseverance* (vv. 2–3). It wasn't a grit-your-teeth-and-bear-it kind of perseverance, but what we could call triumphant fortitude. They stood strong in their community for the cause of Christ and undoubtedly won many victories as a result. The other strength Jesus pointed out was *discerning orthodoxy* (v. 2). They knew Christian doctrine well and had grown able to recognize evil (see Heb. 4:14). Consequently, they did not tolerate people who pretended to be Christians or apostles (compare 2 Cor. 11:12–15, Gal. 1:6–9, 1 Tim. 6:3–5, Titus 1:9–16). False teachers and fake believers were labeled as such by the Ephesian Christians and rendered incapable of doctrinally soiling the church.[4] One can imagine that as the believers in Ephesus heard Christ's commendations, they felt encouraged and proud. However, all was not right.

B. Condemned weakness. After praising their strengths, Jesus told the Ephesians, " 'I have this against you, that you have left your first love' " (v. 4). This statement does not suggest that they no longer had any love for Christ at all. Rather, it means that the quality and intensity of their love for Him had weakened. Just as a wife's love for her husband can become distant and cold with the passing of time, so the Ephesian Christians' love for Christ had waned. Their spiritual fervency was not what it had been, although they had remained active in ministry and orthodox in theology.

IV. Exhortations from the Living Lord

All was not well, but all was not lost. The Ephesian believers could fan the flame of their love for Christ by heeding the counsel at the close of His letter (v. 5). We, too, can rekindle our love for Him if we'll only apply His advice. Let's look at what He suggests.

---

4. Apparently, one such group that the Ephesian Christians identified as heretical—and therefore rightly condemned—were the Nicolaitans (Rev. 2:6). For a more thorough discussion on the identity of the Nicolaitans, see "Revelation," by Johnson, in *The Expositor's Bible Commentary,* p. 435, and *The Book of Revelation,* by Robert H. Mounce (Grand Rapids, Mich.: William B. Eerdmans Publishing Co., 1977), pp. 89–90.

A. Remember. " 'Remember therefore from where you have fallen' " (v. 5a). This could mean, "Recall the time when you began to grow cold toward Me and deal with the cause." If this is what Jesus is saying, then we need to discover where we got sidetracked and do whatever it takes to turn back to Him. Christ may also mean, "Recall the pit from which you were dug." In other words, we should keep in mind the kind of life from which Jesus redeemed us. That will help us rediscover the love we had for Him when we first believed.

B. Repent. This word means "turn back, change your mind, go back" (v. 5b). Without true repentance—a real 180-degree change in direction—we will not regain our loving devotion to Him. And that begins by seeking His forgiveness.

C. Return. " 'Do the deeds you did at first' " (v. 5b). It's never too late to start doing what is right—to begin obeying the Scriptures in the power of the Holy Spirit. If we choose to continue to go the wrong way, we run the risk of losing our effectiveness as beacons of light for Christ (v. 5c). But we do not have to become useless if we will remember, repent, and return.

D. Listen. " 'He who has an ear, let him hear what the Spirit says to the churches' " (v. 7a). Are you listening to God's voice? Are you willing to do what is necessary to warm your heart toward Him again?

E. Believe. " 'To him who overcomes, I will grant to eat of the tree of life, which is in the Paradise of God' " (v. 7b). Christ promises that all those who trust in Him will inherit the blessings of heaven. Do you believe Him? If so, don't live your life with indifference toward Him. Begin to enjoy some of your heavenly inheritance by recommitting yourself to Him now.

 Living Insights

Study One ▬▬▬▬▬▬▬▬▬▬▬▬▬▬▬▬▬▬▬▬▬▬▬▬▬

History tells us that the church in Ephesus was a bastion of orthodoxy—yet it possessed a glaring weakness. Let's make sure we understand the situation.

● What's really being said in this message to the Ephesian church? Write out Revelation 2:1–7 in your notebook, using your own words. This is called *paraphrasing*. It's a great tool for personalizing and clarifying passages of Scripture.

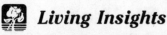

Living Insights

Study Two

Our analysis of the Ephesian Christians fell nicely into three strengths, a weakness, and five exhortations. Let's use this as an opportunity to probe into our own lifestyles.

● How do your strengths compare to the strengths of this church? Check (√) the appropriate responses:

—Energetic, hard-working
☐ Perfectly describes me
☐ In no way describes me
☐ Somewhat describes me

—Patient
☐ Perfectly describes me
☐ In no way describes me
☐ Somewhat describes me

—Discerning
☐ Perfectly describes me
☐ In no way describes me
☐ Somewhat describes me

● Do you suffer from the same weakness—losing your first love?
☐ Yes ☐ No

● Let's take the next few minutes to evaluate. What areas seem to be OK? What areas need work? How can you apply the five exhortations (remember, repent, return, listen, believe) toward improving some of your weaker areas?

When Suffering Strikes

James 1:12, Revelation 2:8–11

It has been said that music is a universal language—so is suffering. Neither require words in order to communicate; both penetrate deeper into our souls than words ever could. However, they do have differences. Music can be enjoyed and appreciated by even the hardest heart. Suffering, on the other hand, is rarely welcomed by anyone—in fact, we'll go to almost any length to avoid it. But there isn't always an escape. It might be possible for us to go through life without ever hearing a note of music. Not so with suffering. No matter how short or long our lives, each of us will experience some degree of affliction. So, how should we handle it when it strikes? Does the Lord give us any counsel? The letter Jesus wrote to the church at Smyrna, the second of the seven first-century churches, reveals some down-to-earth answers to these practical questions.

I. Instruction from a Related Verse

James 1:12 closely ties into the message of Christ's letter to Smyrna: "Blessed is a man who perseveres under trial; for once he has been approved, he will receive the crown of life, which the Lord has promised to those who love Him." There are two main thoughts in this passage. First, when we hang tough through times of trial, we will receive special favor from God—we will be blessed. This divine blessing will consist of an increase in knowledge and growth in spiritual fortitude. Depending on God through suffering brings an understanding about life that we would not otherwise gain. This deeper insight gives us the ability to make some sense out of our anguish and to learn how to be content in spite of it. Second, once our trial is over, we will receive a special reward from God. The reward is called "the crown of life"—a crown that will find its fullest expression in heaven, where those who have chosen to endure for Christ on earth will be rewarded with a special degree of dignity, victory, and happiness. So God gives a two-part blessing to Christians who faithfully endure suffering.[1]

II. Examination of a Personal Letter

What is stated in principle in James 1:12 is illustrated and amplified in practice in Revelation 2:8–11. Let's dig into this passage, opening another personal letter from Jesus Christ.

A. A letter from Christ. Jesus addresses His second letter " 'to the angel [that is, the pastor] of the church in Smyrna' " (v. 8a). Of the seven cities Jesus mentions in His correspondence, only

---

1. For more information on the rewards available to believers, see the study guide *Improving Your Serve: The Art of Unselfish Living,* rev. ed., Bill Watkins, ed., from the Bible-teaching ministry of Charles R. Swindoll (Fullerton, Calif.: Insight for Living, 1986), pp. 76–79.

Smyrna still exists. Today it is called Izmir. The city is one of the largest in modern Turkey, housing a population of a half-million. Two thousand years ago, Smyrna, built on the slopes of Mount Pagus and on the flatland around the nearby harbor, was second only to Ephesus in exports. Described on coins as "First of Asia in beauty and size," it housed the largest public theater in Asia as well as a famous stadium and library.[2] Smyrna had an incredibly strong allegiance to Rome. It was a center for Roman emperor worship, and anyone who refused to publicly confess allegiance to the government was liable to be executed. Smyrna's zealous political loyalty coupled with a small but highly anti-Christian Jewish population made the city an extremely dangerous place for Christians to live. In fact, evidence suggests that life in Smyrna for a faithful Christian was more perilous than it was anywhere else in the Roman Empire.[3] To the believers who resided in this hostile city, Jesus dictated a letter of comfort and encouragement. Even Christ's opening statement of self-identification must have uplifted these persecuted Christians. He said, " '[I am] the first and the last, who was dead, and has come to life' " (v. 8b). Smyrna may have been first in Asia in beauty and size, but Christ—the founder and finisher of the faith—created all the world and will someday judge evil and reward good. Moreover, He once died at the hands of wicked men, yet rose from the grave, conquering death and defeating evil. How comforting these truths must have been to Christians who daily faced the threat of death. Their Savior knew what they were experiencing, and He had the power to see them through it.

B. An explanation of their condition. Next, Jesus mentioned three facts about the state of the church at Smyrna. First, He said that He knew about her tribulation (v. 9a). In classical Greek, the term for *tribulation* paints a picture of a huge rock crushing whatever lies beneath it. The word conveys intense and constant pressure that often leads to death. Jesus was aware that the Christians in Smyrna were literally having the life squeezed out of them. Second, Christ stated that He knew about their deep poverty (v. 9a). Materially, the Christians in Smyrna were destitute, probably because of economic pressure brought to bear by their refusal to participate in emperor worship. However, their

2. Robert H. Mounce, *The Book of Revelation* (Grand Rapids, Mich.: William B. Eerdmans Publishing Co., 1977), p. 91.

3. More background about Smyrna can be found in these sources: *The Letters to the Seven Churches,* by William M. Ramsay (1904; reprint, Grand Rapids, Mich.: Baker Book House, 1985), pp. 251–80; *Archaeology and the New Testament,* by Merrill F. Unger (Grand Rapids, Mich.: Zondervan Publishing House, 1962), pp. 280–82.

economic poverty in no way mirrored their spiritual condition. In their relationship toward God, Christ said they were rich (v. 9a; compare Matt. 6:19–21, 2 Cor. 6:10, James 2:5). Third, the Lord also said He knew about the persecution they were enduring (Rev. 2:9b). This torment came from unsaved Jews who were particularly antagonistic toward Christians. So great was their hostility that Jesus referred to them as " 'a synagogue of Satan' " (v. 9b). They were like the Jews who maligned Jesus during His earthly ministry—who claimed to be descendants of Abraham but revealed by their actions that they were spiritual children of the devil (John 8:39–47).

C. Some encouragement as they suffer. What do you say to believers living under intense persecution, abject poverty, and character assassination? Christ began His words of encouragement with two exhortations. " 'Do not *fear* what you are about to suffer' " was the first (Rev. 2:10a, emphasis added). Just as procrastination is the thief of time, so fear is the thief of peace. Fear stirs up the waters of uncertainty, seriously damages the ship of courage, and can drown sailors of the faith. For the believers in Smyrna, the intimidation factor was especially acute. Not only had they suffered greatly already, but they could anticipate an even greater degree of tribulation—imprisonment and imminent death (v. 10). Jesus knew that as these Christians faced the increasing storm of persecution, fear would be their most formidable enemy. So He urged them to lay their fears aside by *remaining faithful* to Christ, even to the point of death (v. 10b). This was the second command Jesus issued. Their wholehearted trust in Him would help them overcome the debilitating effects of fear, regardless of the affliction brought upon them.

D. Some promises to claim. While exhorting the believers at Smyrna, Christ promised two things. He told them that those who would remain loyal to Him even to death at the executioner's hand would receive " 'the crown of life' " (v. 10b). The archaeologist's spade shows that

> those at Smyrna would be very familiar with the term "the crown of Smyrna," which no doubt alluded to the beautiful skyline formed around the city by the "hill Pagos [sic], with the stately public buildings on its rounded sloping sides" (Ramsay, *Seven Churches,* p. 256). [Moreover,] faithful servants of the city appeared on coins with laurel wreaths on their heads (Barclay, *Seven Churches,* p. 39). As the patriots of Smyrna were faithful to Rome and to their crown city,

so Christ's people are to be faithful unto death to him
who will give them the imperishable crown of life.[4]
Will all Christians receive this wreath of victory? Only those who
faithfully love Christ to the end of their lives will receive this
honor (compare Rev. 2:10 with James 1:12). Jesus also promised
these believers that they would "'not be hurt by the second
death'" (Rev. 2:11b). The first death, of course, is physical. The
second death is spiritual—the everlasting torment reserved for all
fallen angels and those who pass from this life without ever trusting in the Lord as their Savior (2 Pet. 2:4, Jude 6, Rev. 20:10–15).
No Christian will ever experience the second death. Though
believers can lose their rewards, they can never lose their salvation (John 6:37–40, 10:27–30; Rom. 8:1–11, 28–39; 1 Cor. 3:11–15).[5]
This is an encouraging truth to claim, especially when enduring
painful trials and facing the threat of physical death.

III. Application for All Hurting Believers

Unlike the Christians who lived in ancient Smyrna, you may not be
in danger of losing your life for being loyal to Jesus. Instead, you
may be struggling under an unreasonable boss or fighting to keep
a sinking business afloat. Or maybe you are suffering from the verbal
jabs of an uncaring spouse or a rebellious teenager, or you're totter-
ing under pressure from creditors. Regardless of the source of your
hurt or the intensity of your tribulation, there are three principles
grounded in Revelation 2:8–11 on which you can rely.

A. The Lord knows all about your circumstances. You
may feel misunderstood and abandoned, but Jesus knows your
plight, and He will stay with you no matter what. You can count
on that.

B. If things stay the same, Christ will be your fortress.
You have no reason to fear or run. Trust in Him completely, and
He will give you the courage to face your circumstances.

C. If things get worse, the Lord will see you through.
Contrary to popular theology, there are no guarantees that material prosperity and social prestige will come to the faithful in
this life. The Christians who suffered in first-century Smyrna are
a case in point. Indeed, Jesus said their loyalty to Him would lead
to a bleaker situation, not to a better one. Nevertheless, if your
situation goes from bad to worse—and perhaps it already has—

---

4. Alan Johnson, "Revelation," in *The Expositor's Bible Commentary* (Grand Rapids, Mich.:
Regency Reference Library, Zondervan Publishing House, 1981), vol. 12, pp. 438–39.

5. The eternal security of the believer is treated more fully in the study guide *Growing Up in
God's Family,* ed. Bill Watkins, from the Bible-teaching ministry of Charles R. Swindoll
(Fullerton, Calif.: Insight for Living, 1986), p. 57, and in the book *Once Saved, Always Saved,*
by R. T. Kendall (Chicago, Ill.: Moody Press, 1983).

rest in the fact that Christ will give you the strength to endure as you depend on Him. And one day, in front of the vast heavenly host, He will reward you with the crown of life for remaining faithful to Him. No doubt one believer who will get this reward will be Polycarp. He was probably the church leader at Smyrna who received Christ's second letter. Around A.D. 155, Polycarp was brought before the angry citizens of Smyrna and told to swear allegiance to Caesar and blaspheme Christ. The aged bishop refused, answering " 'Eighty and six years have I served him, and he never once wronged me; how then shall I blaspheme my King, Who [has] saved me?' "[6] Even threatened with death by wild beasts, Polycarp remained strong in his stand. Finally, he was warned that if he didn't change his mind, he would be killed by fire. Polycarp replied, " 'You threaten me with fire, which burns for an hour, and is soon extinguished; but the fire of the future judgment, and of eternal punishment reserved for the ungodly, you are ignorant of. But why do you delay? Do whatever you please.' "[7] With this final declaration still ringing in their ears, the Gentiles and Jews of Smyrna together gathered wood on the Jewish Sabbath and used it to burn Polycarp alive. This saint did not bow to the pressure of the moment, even though he faced a horrible death. You, too, can stand up and persevere for Christ, realizing that your "momentary, light affliction is producing for [you] an eternal weight of glory beyond all comparison" (2 Cor. 4:17).

 Living Insights

Study One ■■■

The topic of suffering is not a popular one, but very essential for a Christian to understand. Several biblical writers have addressed this subject, so let's glean some insights from a few of them.

• Paul, James, Peter, and John all commented on endurance through suffering. Copy the following chart into your notebook and read the passages indicated. State principles that could be valuable to a believer going through periods of tribulation. Keep it handy...you never know when you might need it!

6. John Foxe, *Foxe's Book of Martyrs* (Springdale, Penn.: Whitaker House, 1981), p. 22.

7. Foxe, *Foxe's Book of Martyrs,* p. 23.

Writers/References	Principles of Perseverance
Paul (Romans 5:3–5)	
James (James 1:1–12)	
Peter (1 Peter 4:12–19)	
John (Revelation 2:8–11)	

 Living Insights

Study Two ▰▰▰▰▰▰▰▰▰▰▰▰▰▰▰▰▰▰▰▰▰▰▰▰▰

It's one thing to treat suffering as an academic subject. It's quite another to actually deal with it in your own life. Let's do that now.

● Take this time to write an essay. Title it "Suffering and My Life." Perhaps you would like to address these issues: Why do I suffer? Why *don't* I suffer? What have I learned from past difficulties? Could these lessons have been learned through other means? How do I perceive my sufferings in relation to others' hardships? What place do I *really* give God during difficult times?

Ministering Where Satan Dwells
Revelation 2:12–17

The church in Ephesus was orthodox, active, and wise, yet lacked a warm love for Christ. Assaulted and poverty-stricken, the church in Smyrna suffered greatly, yet still remained faithful to the Lord. The third church Christ addressed was the church at Pergamum, located in a city referred to as the dwelling place of Satan (Rev. 2:13). Needless to say, it was an extremely tough city for a Christian to live and minister in. Unfortunately, the believers in Pergamum did not rise to the occasion and shine brightly for Christ, but allowed their witness to diminish to a mere flicker. How? By compromising their godly standards with the godlessness of their culture. Like many of us today, they fell prey to one of Satan's most devious methods of rendering God's people spiritually ineffective. Knowing of their compromise with evil, Christ sent them a letter that directly confronted their sin and indirectly alerts us to the same danger. Let's remain vulnerable to His piercing words concerning compromise.

I. Description of the Judge

As with the other letters in Revelation 2–3, the letter to the church in Pergamum is addressed to its pastor (2:12a). However, the One who dictates this third letter describes Himself differently than He does in the first two. Christ says that He is " 'the One who has the sharp two-edged sword' " (v. 12b). The image of this sword probably has a double reference—one theological and the other cultural. From a doctrinal perspective, the sword likely represents the Bible as the penetrating Word of God (compare Heb. 4:12). The emphasis on its double-edged sharpness probably indicates Scripture's ability "to judge the thoughts and intentions of the heart" (v. 12b). It is God's written standard of perfection; consequently, it is capable of revealing truth and error, right and wrong, regardless of how foggy the issues become to us. From a cultural viewpoint, the sword imagery may be communicating that like Pergamum—a city that was given the power of the sword—Christ has power over life and death. But unlike Pergamum, Jesus' authority is ultimate—not granted by Rome or limited by civil boundaries. His legal right to judge is inherent, coming straight from His mouth (Rev. 1:16; 19:15, 21), and His authority is universal, since it is grounded in His limitless divine nature.

II. Condition of the Church

Christ's letter to the believers in Pergamum continues, first with words of praise and then with words of criticism.

A. Commendable factors. Jesus first tells the Pergamum Christians that He knows about their city, " 'where Satan's throne is' "

(2:13a). Some background information on Pergamum is needed to understand what Christ is saying. The city was "situated on a hill about one thousand feet high and eighteen miles from the Aegean [Sea]."[1] From this strategic position, Pergamum controlled "the fertile valley of the Caicus River and a land route into the interior of Asia Minor."[2] This city was known for its magnificent architecture and great library, which was second only to the world-famous library in Alexandria, Egypt. Pergamum was most renowned, however, not as an economic or cultural center but as a flourishing center of pagan worship. In 29 B.C., it became "the first city of Asia to receive permission [from Rome] to build a temple dedicated to the worship of a living [human] ruler."[3] Within a brief period of time, Pergamum "had three temples in which Roman emperors were worshiped as gods."[4] Other deities, such as Zeus, Athena, Dionysos, and Asklepios, were worshiped in Pergamum as well. Each major god had a temple, and each center of worship was lavishly decorated and ornately sculptured. In fact, Zeus's altar was so superb that it was named among the Seven Wonders of the World. There is little doubt that Pergamum's saturation with idolatry led Christ to refer to the city as a major seat of satanic influence. And perhaps the god of Pergamum that best epitomized Jesus' comment was Asklepios, the god of healing, whose symbol was a serpent and who was referred to as Savior.[5] On some coins of Pergamum, this deity was shown "coiled around a bending sapling" in front of a Roman emperor who had "his right hand [raised] in the exact gesture of the Nazi salute, which is . . . one of the most ancient of all gestures of adoration."[6] The symbol of a snake would have readily reminded Christians of their greatest spiritual adversary—the devil (compare Gen. 3:1–5; Eph. 6:11–16; Rev. 12:9, 20:1–2). The mere fact that the believers at Pergamum had chosen to remain in Satan's eastern Roman stronghold was amazing. Indeed, we may detect from the words in the beginning of Revelation 2:13 Christ's implicit commendation to these disciples for not running

1. Howard F. Vos, *Archaeology in Bible Lands* (Chicago, Ill.: Moody Press, 1977), p. 329.

2. Vos, *Archaeology in Bible Lands,* p. 329.

3. Robert H. Mounce, *The Book of Revelation* (Grand Rapids, Mich.: William B. Eerdmans Publishing Co., 1977), p. 96.

4. Merrill F. Unger, *Archaeology and the New Testament* (Grand Rapids, Mich.: Zondervan Publishing House, 1962), p. 277.

5. See E. M. Blaiklock's *The Archaeology of the New Testament,* rev. ed. (Nashville, Tenn.: Thomas Nelson Publishers, 1984), p. 127, and Mounce's *The Book of Revelation,* p. 95.

6. Blaiklock, *The Archaeology of the New Testament,* p. 127.

from a religiously hostile community. Explicitly, the Lord praised these Christians for holding fast to His name and not denying the faith (v. 13a). They had remained loyal to Christ by refusing to bow to the intense pressure to worship false gods. Even when one of their own members, Antipas, was killed for his commitment to Christ, the believers in Pergamum did not crumble but stood undaunted in their faith (v. 13b).[7]

B. Condemnable problems. Although these first-century believers were strong in some areas, they were terribly weak in others. Jesus singles out two problems which expose the fact that the Pergamum church was divided by compromise in both doctrine and practice.

1. **The Balaamite heresy.** According to Numbers 22–25 and 31, the prophet Balaam showed King Balak how he could use the Moabite women to seduce the Israelite men into sexual immorality, illegal intermarriage, and pagan worship. Balaam's plan was successful; thus, the prophet "became a prototype of all corrupt teachers who betrayed believers into fatal compromise with worldly ideologies."[8] Christ states that some of the church members at Pergamum had succumbed to the deception of Balaam (Rev. 2:14). They had taken a middle course that led them astray from their Christian mores. In their case, deterioration began with their participation in the meals that were commonly held to honor heathen gods (v. 14b). The food served at these celebrations was frequently the leftovers of pagan sacrifices. By eating this food, the Christians were becoming "sharers in demons" (1 Cor. 10:20). Furthermore, involvement in these pagan festivities made it easier to indulge in sexual intercourse with temple priestesses who prostituted themselves for the gods they served (Rev. 2:14b). In short, some of the Pergamum Christians had compromised their faith by allowing themselves to mix it with pagan practices.

2. **The Nicolaitan heresy.** The word *thus* at the beginning of Revelation 2:15 strongly indicates that the Nicolaitan and Balaamite heresies were closely linked. Indeed, even the terms Nicolaitan and Balaam can mean the same thing—

---

7. An interesting sidelight to this point is provided by Mounce: "[New Testament scholar] Zahn notes that under [the emperor] Diocletian, Christian stone cutters from Rome working in the quarries of Pannonia refused to carve an image of Aesculapius (Latin designation of Asklepios) and consequently were put to death for being followers of Antipas of Pergamum" (*The Book of Revelation*, p. 96, fn. 36).

8. Mounce, *The Book of Revelation*, p. 98.

namely, "conquer the people."[9] Many commentators view the Nicolaitans as a Christian group that abused their freedom in Christ by accommodating their doctrine and conduct to the society in which they lived. Some of the believers in Pergamum certainly fit into the Nicolaitan camp. Their moral laxness and religious syncretism made them tragic adherents of this ancient heresy. For this also, Christ criticized them.

III. Correction of Compromise

Fortunately, the problems of the Pergamum believers were not insurmountable. Their solution lay in one act—repentance (v. 16a). Short of death, that's the only way to end an affair with compromise. We must return to seeing the situation through God's eyes and begin responding to it according to the principles revealed in His Word. Put another way, we must change our minds so we can change our wills and thereby change our lives. That's what repentance is all about. But what if we decide to keep compromising? Then Christ's " 'or else' " to the believers in Pergamum becomes His plan of attack for us: " 'I am coming to you quickly, and I will make war against them with the sword of My mouth' " (v. 16b). The change from *you* to *them* indicates that Jesus will not wage war on all Christians in a church marked by disobedience. Rather, He will severely judge those who are personally involved in tolerating theological or practical compromise. To them, His written standard of truth and morality will become a means of condemnation rather than encouragement. It will become a sword that cuts instead of one that heals. Perhaps, also, Christ will exercise His authority over life against compromisers by making them weak or ill or even by removing them from the earth (compare 1 Cor. 11:27–34). However He chooses to respond, we may be assured that He will not put up with Christians who defile His name either directly or indirectly, actively or passively.

IV. Restoration of Compromisers

What if we choose to repent of the bargains we've made with false doctrines and immoral practices? What will Christ do then? He promises that He will do three things. First, He " 'will give [us] some of the hidden manna' " (Rev. 2:17b). He will nourish us with spiritual food that unbelievers do not know about or see. This manna will come from His Word and be made effective in our lives through the ministry of His Holy Spirit. Second, the Lord " 'will give [us] a white stone' " (v. 17b). This image likely refers to the ancient judicial practice of jurors casting their vote for acquittal by casting a white pebble

9. See Alan Johnson's "Revelation," in *The Bible Expositor's Commentary* (Grand Rapids, Mich.: Regency Reference Library, Zondervan Publishing House, 1981), vol. 12, p. 441.

into an urn.[10] In other words, our repentance will bring Christ's vote of forgiveness—an act that removes the guilt and stigma attached to compromise. Third, Jesus promises that He will give us "'a new name written on the stone which no one knows but he who receives it'" (v. 17b). He'll change our faithlessness into faithfulness, our dishonesty into honesty, our impurity into purity. When we turn our backs on compromise, He begins to cleanse us, restore us, and reform us. What more could we ask for?

V. Some Closing Thoughts on Compromise

How can we keep ourselves free from unhealthy compromise? Recalling these three facts will help.

A. It never occurs quickly. Compromise cuts its eye inconspicuously and inoffensively. It begins with a second glance... leads to flirtation... to a first touch... then finally and fatally to unfaithfulness. We need to stop glancing over our shoulders at sin; we need to look forward, instead, and keep the standards of God's Word in clear view.

B. It always lowers the original standard. Compromise never exalts, only lowers; it never uplifts, only debases; it never enhances morality, only effaces it. Watch out for concessions to God's biblical standards. They will inevitably lead to sin and guilt.

C. It is often the first step toward total disobedience. Compromise is like a slippery slope—once you start sliding, it's extremely difficult to stop. Fortunately, however, with God's help and a repentant spirit, compromise can be stopped in its tracks. Do you struggle with compromise? Are you slipping down its slope right now? If so, plant your feet firmly in the mountain of God's mercy. Repent. Turn away from your sin. And claim His promises of forgiveness and renewal.

 Living Insights

Study One ━━━━━━━━━━━━━━━━━━━━━━━━━━━━━━━━━━━━━━

The New Testament often refers to passages from the Old Testament. In order to fully understand the New Testament passage, it's vital to first understand the point of the Old Testament reference. Today's text is a good example.

• Revelation 2:14 states that the church at Pergamum was following the "teaching of Balaam." Turn to Numbers 22–25 and read about

---

10. See *The Revelation of Jesus Christ,* by John F. Walvoord (Chicago, Ill.: Moody Press, 1966), pp. 70–71.

this Old Testament prophet. How would you describe the "teaching of Balaam"? What was Balaam's mistake?

- Let's make the transition to the Pergamum church. How did Balaam's teaching manifest itself in this particular church? Using what you've learned, rephrase the Lord's warning in Revelation 2:14.

 Living Insights

Study Two

Compromise . . . what thoughts are conjured up in your mind by that word? Whatever your definition, in the context of the Pergamum church it was certainly less than desirable. How about areas of compromise in your life?

- In what areas are you susceptible to compromise? Write a little self-evaluation for each of the categories below.
—Doctrine
—Finances
—Marriage
—Honesty
—Business
—Sex
—Morals
—Other _____
- God's advice for those in compromise is: *Stop!* Spend a few minutes in prayer, asking God for wisdom in purifying these areas of your life.

Jezebel in the Church
Revelation 2:18–29

Of the seven churches Christ addresses in Revelation 2–3, the church at Thyatira was located in "the least known, least important, and least remarkable of the cities."[1] Thyatira was to Ephesus what Flat Creek, Tennessee is to Los Angeles, California, or what Cut-'n-Shoot, Texas is to Chicago, Illinois. It couldn't compare with the size, beauty, and importance of the other Asian cities. Militarily, it was expendable, founded as a buffer zone designed to slow down advancing armies. Politically and culturally, the city was nothing special. It seems that its only claim to fame was that, though small, it was a prosperous manufacturing and marketing center. It had numerous highly organized trade guilds concerned with commerce in wool, linen, dyed material, clothing, leatherwork, baked goods, pottery, bronze work, and slaves. "Each guild had its own patron deity, feasts, and seasonal festivities that included sexual revelries."[2] Why did Christ address a letter to this rather obscure town? And why did He preserve it for our eyes? The letter's content suggests at least two reasons. One was to encourage all believers who live and minister in small, out-of-the-way places. The other was to warn all churches about the consequences of tolerating a Jezebel in their midst. Let's open our Bibles to this personal letter and consider what it says to us.

I. The Judge Described
Jesus identifies Himself as " 'the Son of God, who has eyes like a flame of fire, and His feet are like burnished bronze' " (Rev. 2:18). Christ's unequivocal and immediate claim of deity shows that He needed to assert His authority in a stronger manner with the church in Thyatira than with the previous three churches He addressed. The mention of flaming eyes suggests "the penetrating power of Christ's ability to see through the seductive arguments of Jezebel and those who were being led astray by her pernicious teaching. Feet . . . like burnished brass convey the idea of strength and splendor."[3] Jesus was writing as Thyatira's sovereign Lord and Judge, and He expected the members of this church to perk up their ears—to listen carefully and fearfully.

II. The Church Revealed
As He did with the churches in Ephesus and Pergamum, Christ first commended, then criticized the church at Thyatira.

1. Hemer, as quoted by Robert H. Mounce in *The Book of Revelation* (Grand Rapids, Mich.: William B. Eerdmans Publishing Co., 1977), p. 101.

2. Alan Johnson, "Revelation," in *The Expositor's Bible Commentary* (Grand Rapids, Mich.: Regency Reference Library, Zondervan Publishing House, 1981), vol. 12, p. 443.

3. Mounce, *The Book of Revelation,* p. 102.

A. Its strengths recognized. Jesus praised the church's virtues—namely, her love, faith, service, and perseverance (v. 19a). He also spoke highly of her enthusiastic growth in living out her faith (v. 19b). Unlike the Ephesian church, who had lost her zealous devotion to Christ, the church at Thyatira was steadily becoming a blazing fire in her commitment to Him.

An Exhortation to Affirm

As we'll soon see, Jesus saw a serious flaw in the Thyatiran church. However, before He confronted her weakness, He affirmed her strengths. He realized that the Christians in this church needed His encouragement as much as they needed His rebuke. Do you know someone who has become demoralized, depressed, or frustrated? Perhaps this person is wrestling with a difficult problem, or maybe just feels unappreciated. Whatever the case, take some time to encourage that person. Pick up the phone, write a letter— better yet, drop by for a friendly visit. Give this individual some positive strokes rather than negative jabs. And even if you must confront some wrong, preface your rebuke with words of acceptance and affirmation. This will be the spoonful of sugar to help the medicine go down more easily. Remember, "a man has joy in an apt answer, / And how delightful is a timely word!" (Prov. 15:23; compare v. 30).

B. Its weakness addressed. Following Jesus' commendations came His criticism: " 'I have this against you, that you tolerate the woman Jezebel, who calls herself a prophetess, and she teaches and leads My bond-servants astray, so that they commit acts of immorality and eat things sacrificed to idols. And I gave her time to repent; and she does not want to repent of her immorality' " (Rev. 2:20–21). Let's examine this rebuke.

  1. **The object of the reprimand.** Interestingly enough, Jesus directed His rebuke against the Thyatiran church, not Jezebel. He was angry that the believers in this church had tolerated false teaching and sinful behavior rather than confronting and condemning them.

  2. **The source of the problem.** Christ identified the origin of the church's troubles as a self-proclaimed prophetess called Jezebel. Several identifications have been proposed for Jezebel. Some commentators have suggested that she was the wife of the church's pastor, since the Greek word for *woman* in Revelation 2:20 may also mean "wife." This identification is highly unlikely, since the possessive pronoun for *your* does

not appear with *woman* in the best and earliest manuscripts of this passage. Others have claimed that Jezebel was Lydia, the woman Paul converted in Philippi (Acts 16:14–15). There is no substantial reason for accepting this identification. Some other expositors have interpreted Jezebel as a metaphor of conformity to heathen standards. However, there is nothing in Christ's words that clearly suggests we should view Jezebel as a mere symbol. The more natural interpretation of the passage is that Jezebel was a real woman in the church at Thyatira who claimed to have the gift of prophecy. It is feasible, however, that this woman's name was not really Jezebel. Like the name Judas, the name Jezebel had negative connotations for the Thyatiran Christians. Therefore, it may be that she was called Jezebel by Christ because He saw qualities in her that resembled those of the Jezebel of Old Testament fame, who was the Canaanite wife of Israel's King Ahab. She led Ahab away from worshiping God to serve the false god Baal. Then, through intimidation and deception, she got her husband to promulgate her idolatrous teachings throughout Israel (1 Kings 16:31–33, 2 Kings 9:22). Considering her life, we can come up with four characteristics of a Jezebel-like person: (1) cleverly deceptive, (2) manipulatively dominant, (3) viciously scheming, and (4) influentially wicked. Apparently, the woman who was active in the church at Thyatira manifested such traits. She used her powers of persuasion to lead some of the congregation to participate in pagan feasts and sexual promiscuity. Although Christ gave her time to repent of her wicked deeds, she refused, continuing to spread her poison throughout the church without receiving any significant opposition. No wonder the Lord was angry!

III. The Judgment Proclaimed

The verdict was in. The church was guilty of tolerating sin in her ranks, and the "prophetess" was guilty of promoting sin in the church. Thus, Christ rendered His judgment. He would make the woman physically ill, and He would bring great suffering or even death to those who joined with her in adulterating their relationship with the Lord (Rev. 2:22–23a; compare 1 Cor. 11:27–30). The wording of Christ's punishment indicates that the woman's disciples still had time to repent, while she did not. Jesus made it clear that none of the guilty would escape His judgment. He " 'searches the minds and hearts' " and either rewards or punishes people according to their deeds (Rev. 2:23b; compare Heb. 4:13, Matt. 16:27, Rom. 2:6).

IV. The Faithful Encouraged

To those who refused to be swayed by the Jezebel-like teaching—doctrines referred to as "the deep things of Satan"—Jesus said that they would not be given any other burden (Rev. 2:24). The faithful Christians at Thyatira had only one burden: obedience to God. Christ knew that their commitment to obedience in a culture that promoted immoral living was hard work. He encouraged them to keep at it until He would come again to give them authority to rule with Him in His millennial kingdom (vv. 25–28; compare Matt. 25:14–23, Rev. 20:4).

V. The Truth Applied

There are many truths in this ancient letter that reach across the centuries into ours with eager hands of application. Let's focus our attention on four of them.

A. **Big problems can occur in little places; don't be surprised.** Wherever there are people, there are sinners. They don't need a large city or church in which to disobey God.

B. **Timely words can encourage demoralized people; don't be hesitant.** Like you, others need affirming words and friendly embraces. Don't wait until tomorrow to uplift other people. Start making it a habitual part of your life today.

C. **Wrong teaching can come from gifted individuals; don't be misled.** Attractive, winsome, talented people are not necessarily infallible intellectually or morally. Indeed, many have used their charisma to lure people away from a godly lifestyle. Stay on your guard! Consistently test the claims of others against the clear teaching of God's Word (Gal. 1:6–9, 1 John 4:1–6).

D. **Deceptive actions can hurt even the innocent; don't be stubborn.** If you're engaged in leading people astray or in deceiving others in any way, *stop it now!* Repent. Set the record straight. Receive God's forgiveness. Return to the right track. If you don't, Christ will eventually expose and discipline you. Don't kid yourself. The Lord will not tolerate sin forever. His patience has limits, and when it runs out, judgment comes rolling down like raging waters (Amos 5:24, 1 Pet. 3:9–12).

 Living Insights

Study One

Our study has revealed that Thyatira was quite a small town in comparison to the cities studied previously. Most likely Christ's letter made quite a stir in this tiny hamlet!

Continued on next page

- You're a cub reporter with the *Thyatira Times*. The editor hands you this letter as your assignment. He wants you to write a story using the most basic journalism technique—asking the right questions: who, what, where, when, why, and how. Submit Revelation 2:18–29 to those questions and write your story based on your understanding of the facts.

Living Insights

Study Two

Do you feel like one of the citizens of Thyatira? This study concluded with four practical truths to apply and remember. Why not use these four principles as catalysts for your thinking.

- Gather family or close friends and talk about incidents you've experienced or observed that relate to these truths—or just reminisce a little by yourself. Which principle hits closest to home in your life? Close with a time of affirmation and prayer.
  —Big problems can occur in little places; don't be surprised.
  —Timely words can encourage demoralized people; don't be hesitant.
  —Wrong teaching can come from gifted individuals; don't be misled.
  —Deceptive actions can hurt even the innocent; don't be stubborn.

A Morgue with a Steeple
Revelation 3:1–6

Between the fourteenth and sixteenth centuries, committed Christians such as John Wycliffe, Martin Luther, and John Calvin challenged the European church to return to her spiritual roots and once again become a vital force for Christ in the world. By the mid-1800s, however, the great accomplishments of the Protestant Reformation had lost much of their impact. Indeed, they were in the process of being buried beneath the dirt of religious formalism and complacency. The church was not confronting and reforming her culture; instead, she had become an innocuous extension of European society itself. The secularization of the church led atheist philosopher Friedrich Nietzsche to herald God's death. As far as he could see, Europe no longer needed to lean on the Christian concept of God. God was culturally dead, and churches were merely His tombs and monuments.[1] Another philosopher, Soren Kierkegaard, saw the same problem, but reached a much different conclusion. Kierkegaard passionately urged his lethargic brothers to renew their commitment to Christ, regardless of the cultural conflicts it might create for them.[2] The situation was nothing new. The Church had faced secularization centuries before, in ancient Sardis. But in Sardis, no one rose up to confront it. Jesus Christ Himself had to meet it head-on, and He did so in His letter to that church. His words to the Christians there apply just as much now to congregations and individuals who appear to be spiritually alive, but inside are spiritually dead.

I. The Condition

This fifth letter from Christ begins like the others. It's addressed to the head teacher or minister of the church at Sardis (Rev. 3:1a) and contains Jesus' opening statement of identification. This time, however, He refers to Himself as the One " 'who has the seven Spirits of God, and the seven stars' " (v. 1b). The seven stars, of course, stand for the pastors of the seven churches (compare 1:20). The identity of the seven Spirits is not as obvious. Many Bible scholars think that the phrase refers to Isaiah 11:2–5, where seven characteristics of the Holy Spirit are listed as resting upon Christ.[3] Others interpret the description "as a symbolic or allegorical way of expressing the full range of exercise of the Divine power in the Seven Churches."[4]

1. Friedrich Nietzsche, "The Joyful Wisdom," as presented in *Reality, Man, and Existence: Essential Works of Existentialism,* ed. H. J. Blackham (New York, N.Y.: Bantam Books, 1965), pp. 66–67.

2. See Soren Kierkegaard's books *Attack Upon Christendom* (Boston, Mass.: Beacon Press, 1957), and *Fear and Trembling* (Princeton, N.J.: Princeton University Press, 1954).

3. See John F. Walvoord, *The Revelation of Jesus Christ* (Chicago, Ill.: Moody Press, 1966), p. 79.

4. William M. Ramsay, *The Letters to the Seven Churches* (1904; reprint, Grand Rapids, Mich.: Baker Book House, 1985), p. 370.

Whatever the meaning, it's clear that the sender of the letter is Christ. Since He is the ultimate Head not only of the church in Sardis but of all the churches in the world, we need to listen intently to what He has to say.

A. The church at Sardis. Jesus goes right to the point: " 'I know your deeds, that you have a name that you are alive, but you are dead' " (v. 1b). Anyone peeping into the windows of the church at Sardis would have seen its members praying, singing, and listening to God's Word. They would probably have walked away thinking, "Now there's a church alive for Christ!" But they would have been wrong. The church at Sardis was a morgue with a steeple. She seemed healthy enough on the outside, but on the inside she was dead. The church had become like the city in which she resided. At one time, Sardis was the capital of the great kingdom of Lydia. An extremely wealthy city, it has been given credit for making the first coins and for popularizing the dyeing of wool. The original section of Sardis was practically impregnable, built on a rock that towered more than one thousand feet above the broad, fertile river basin of the Hermus. The city was constantly in a state of moral and religious corruption—its citizens were known for combining wild sexual orgies with their worship of heathen gods. The people were self-indulgent and self-satisfied; consequently, they had "the peace of the man whose dreams are dead and whose mind is asleep, the peace of lethargy and evasion."[5] One historian summed up ancient Sardis this way:

> No city in the whole province of Asia had a more splendid history in past ages than Sardis. No city of Asia at that time showed such a melancholy contrast between past splendour and present decay as Sardis. Its history was the exact opposite of . . . Smyrna. Smyrna was dead and yet lived. Sardis lived and yet was dead.[6]

The church in Sardis had once been a faithful, loving servant of Christ—but no more. In the past she had been the city's conscience—but no more. She began to revel in her past accomplishments while living in comfortable coexistence with her pagan neighbors. She became the nice, harmless church on the corner . . . in religious activity, benignly alive; in spiritual vitality, malignantly dead.

B. Some reasons for spiritual death. We don't know specifically what caused the death of the church at Sardis, but we do

---

5. William Barclay, *Letters to the Seven Churches,* as quoted by Alan Johnson in "Revelation," from *The Expositor's Bible Commentary* (Grand Rapids, Mich.: Regency Reference Library, Zondervan Publishing House, 1981), vol. 12, p. 448.

6. Ramsay, *The Letters to the Seven Churches,* p. 375.

know some potential killers of vibrant congregations. Let's get acquainted with five of them.

1. **Worship of the past.** A church that continually looks back— continually talks about "the way we were"—is on its way to dying. Churches need to understand where they have been so they can get a better idea about where they should go and how they should get there. Learning from the past and living in the past are really two different things. *Learning* from the past leads to healthy change. But *living* in the lap of its past history, a church can die.

2. **Greater concern with cosmetics than with character.** How ministry is carried out is important—a church that wants to be on the cutting edge of effective ministry must consider its methods. But when finding the best method becomes more consuming than developing Christian character, paralysis creeps in. If the process continues, a church ends up with spiritual invalids trying to run the marathon of ministry—a certain formula for failure.

3. **Love of tradition over love for Christ.** Change is a fact of life—no one understands this better than those who work closely with young people. Churches that relinquish worn-out ways of doing things stand a good chance of remaining viable instruments for Christ, especially among teenagers. But congregations that are tradition-bound are likely to slowly sink into a sea of irrelevance, rendering themselves incapable of reaching out to contemporary youth.

4. **Inflexibility and resistance to change.** Though churches are to be committed to a centuries-old book called the Bible, they are not to be inflexible in their application of its truths. Cultures, attitudes, beliefs, circumstances . . . they all change, though God's Word does not. This demands that congregations seek out new ways to communicate and apply timeless principles without compromising the divine standard that undergirds and informs them. If churches fail to do this, they will inevitably find that they are talking to no one but themselves.

5. **Losing evangelistic and missionary fervor.** Another sure way to kill a church is to turn it into a closed community . . . one interested only in the development of its members. This type of spiritual self-indulgence actually stunts—even reverses—individual as well as church growth. What else could we expect? Evangelism is one of the sparks that preserves the flame. When that is removed, the fire dies. Closed doors breed suffocation.

II. The Correction

Identifying a problem is the first step toward solving it. The problem with the church at Sardis was that she was dead. But as hopeless as that sounds, all was not lost. Jesus saw the glow of embers among the ashes and exhorted the believers in Sardis to fan the flame with renewed commitment to Him. How could they do this? What steps were they to take? Christ gave them five directives that, if obeyed, would burn new life into their church.

A. Wake up! In the original Greek text, Christ's first command literally says "Be constantly alert" (v. 2a). Apparently, the believers had become so self-centered and spiritually sluggish that they didn't realize what desperate straits they were in. Jesus wanted them to open their eyes and take a critical look at their condition. Have you taken a good look at your *own* spiritual condition lately? Do you do this often?[7]

B. Strengthen the remnant. For all practical purposes, the church at Sardis was dead, but she was still able to be resuscitated. A few individuals remained within her walls who had enough life left to break death's stranglehold. Jesus exhorted these breathing believers to shake some life into their brothers (v. 2b). The church had become lackadaisical in her responsibilities, not because of persecution or the adoption of heresy, but because of her contentment with mediocrity and former glory. Are you basking in the past rather than living in the present and pressing forward to the future? Have your enthusiasm and conviction begun to wane? If so, take stock of the good that remains and begin to develop it with God's strength.

C. Remember your purpose. Christ put it this way: " 'Remember . . . what you have received and heard' " (v. 3a). The believers at Sardis had received the gospel. They had accepted Christ by faith, been forgiven of their sins, and been granted divine power to live the Christian life. They had also been told what a difference these things should make in their lives. God had lifted them from the mire of sin so they could carry out His perfect will, performing good works zealously (Eph. 2:10, Titus 2:14). We were saved not just to keep us from hell but to orient our lives around heaven— to be like Christ, who came not to be served but to serve.

D. Apply the truth. It's one thing to recall the truths of the faith; it's quite another to apply them to life. Jesus commanded the Christians in Sardis to put their faith into practice—to use it to shape their thinking, direct their goals, mold their attitudes,

---

7. A helpful source for understanding and evaluating Christian growth is the study guide *Growing Up in God's Family,* ed. Bill Watkins, from the Bible-teaching ministry of Charles R. Swindoll (Fullerton, Calif.: Insight for Living, 1986).

channel their emotions, and guide their behavior. Christianity was not simply to *inform* them, but to *transform* their every thought, word, and deed. Are you a different kind of spouse, parent, employee, or friend because of your faith? Do others see the difference in your life without being told you're a Christian?

E. Change your direction. Finally, Jesus urged the believers at Sardis to repent (Rev. 3:3). This is the last exhortation, but it's the one that sets the other four in motion. Without individuals changing their minds and hearts—choosing to recommit themselves to Christ-centered living—the church was doomed. But with repentance, new life would come . . . life that would spread from the individuals to the church as a whole. Are you suffering from the Sardian plague? Do you know that if it goes untreated, it renders its victims spiritually useless? If you have this fatal disease, seek out the divine Physician and follow His prescription for recovery. Then, and only then, will the sickness ebb and health flow through your soul and witness. Remember, the Christian life involves two essentials: (1) the ability to make clear-cut decisions at crucial times, and (2) the ability to carry out those decisions when the going gets tough. God gives these capabilities to those He saves. So, if you're a child of His, step out and use the resources He has given you. He's waiting to forgive, forget, and empower.

A Strong Warning to the Hesitant and Obstinate

Jesus knew that the people of Sardis had a history of smugness that left them vulnerable to attack. Twice the city had been unexpectedly infiltrated and conquered. Each time, the attackers used obscure cracks in the steep mountain walls to scale the cliff and slip into an unguarded portion of the city. Apparently, the city's inhabitants were unaware of the weakness in their fortifications; they thought their city was impervious to attack.[8] This attitude had also penetrated the church. Blind to the cracks in their faith, the Christians in Sardis had allowed the enemies of self-indulgence, indifference, and mediocrity to assault and imprison them. Jesus warned that if they hesitated or refused to take the prescribed actions to free themselves and conquer their assailants, He would come to them in judgment at a time they would not expect (v. 3b). His warning reveals to us that we dare not take Him for granted. He loves His own people so intensely that He will do whatever it takes to

---

8. See Ramsay's *The Letters to the Seven Churches,* pp. 360–62, 376–78, and Johnson's "Revelation," p. 447.

uproot sin from their lives. Are you harboring impurities? Heed Christ's warning, remembering that "it is a terrifying thing to fall into the hands of the living God" (Heb. 10:31).

III. Three Promises for the Faithful

For those Christians who remain faithful and for the others who repent, Jesus gives three promises that span the centuries.

A. Everlasting righteousness. When we become Christ's followers, the Lord begins to purify us until we can stand before Him stripped of sin and clothed in white (Rev. 3:5a).

B. Everlasting citizenship. Our faith commitment to Jesus also brings His assurance that He will never blot out our names from the book of life (v. 5b; compare Dan. 12:1–2, Luke 10:19–20, Rev. 20:15). Our citizenship in heaven is forever secure.

C. Everlasting affirmation. Christ further promises that our loyalty to Him on earth will be rewarded by Him in heaven (Rev. 3:5b; compare Matt. 10:32, Luke 18).

 Living Insights

Study One

A very important point in this study is the significance of *applying the truth.* That's the whole purpose of Living Insights. Let's not allow this opportunity to pass by. Let's apply the truth.

- Like Revelation 3:16, Ezekiel 33:22–33 contains the story of people who heard the truth but didn't bother to apply it. Copy this chart into your notebook. As you read the story in Ezekiel, list some dangers of neglecting application.

References	Dangers of Neglecting Application

🐎 Living Insights

What has been your experience with churches that are spiritually lifeless? Let's look at some signs of death in the church and encourage our congregations to become committed to life.

- **Worship of the past:** How does this manifest itself in a church? What are some warning signs? How can you deal with this if it's already infected your church?
- **Greater concern with cosmetics than with character:** How does a church become susceptible to this threat? What are the differences between "form" and "life"? Be specific.
- **Love of tradition over love for Christ:** Can you think of historical examples to illustrate this principle? Name a few. What lessons can we learn from these past mistakes?
- **Inflexibility and resistance to change:** What's the hardest aspect of dealing with "we've-always-done-it-this-way" thinking? Does it necessarily come with age? How can it be prevented?
- **Loss of evangelistic and missionary fervor:** Is this a common problem? What brings it on? Can we have evangelistic rallies and missions programs and still have the problem?

Open-Door Revival
Revelation 3:7–13

Closed doors are like roadblocks. They shout "Stop! Keep out! Go away!" In churches, closed doors bar outreach for Christ. Open doors, on the other hand, invite exploration and present opportunities for Christians to serve. But by their very nature, open doors of ministry are useless if believers are not ready and willing to walk through them. In the first century A.D., Christ called attention to a church in Asia Minor who proved she was prepared and available for ministry. As a result, the Lord gave her immeasurable opportunities to reach out in His name. What an enviable responsibility! And it's available to us—if we will first open ourselves to Him as the church in Philadelphia did. Let's learn more about this Christian assembly by focusing on the letter she received from the Lord.

I. The Savior Described

Instead of signing His name at the end of the letter, Jesus identified Himself at the beginning: " 'He who is holy, who is true, who has the key of David, who opens and no one will shut, and who shuts and no one opens" (Rev. 3:7b). Let's look at the three attributes Christ used to describe Himself.

A. Holiness. This characteristic has a two-fold meaning with one basic idea—that of being set apart, or separate. Christ's holiness signifies that He is separate from creation. He is not a created being but the Creator of all things (John 1:1–3). Therefore, He is not to be identified or confused with the natural world in any way (compare Exod. 20:4, Deut. 4:9–24). His holiness also means that He is separate from all evil. Even though He died for sinners, He Himself never sinned (1 Pet. 2:21–22). He was and is completely free of all moral contamination and corruption. It's in this sense that He exhorts us to be set apart, or holy (1 Pet. 1:14–16).

B. Veracity. The Greek word *true* also has a double meaning. In one sense, it means "genuine, real." Jesus is the real Lord and Messiah; all others who claim to be Christ are deceivers (Matt. 24:4–5, 23–24). The other definition of the term is "trustworthy, reliable." Jesus can neither lie nor lead people astray (Titus 1:2, Heb. 6:17–18). Therefore, we can count on Him . . . believe everything He says . . . trust His every promise.

Advice for Pretenders

We all tend to put on masks to hide who we really are. At the base of this pretense is fear—fear that leads to countless problems. Tim Hansel put his finger on several of them when he wrote:

> Afraid to fail, we no longer risk. Afraid that some-
> one will see behind our image, we no longer
> share. Afraid that we will appear to need help,
> we can no longer be vulnerable. Afraid to appear
> not religious enough to some, we no longer can
> confess. We withdraw into a petty world con-
> sumed in emptiness and fear, covered with the
> thick shell, worshiping an impotent God. The
> tragic result . . . is that in our fear of becoming
> childlike, in our fear of becoming a fool for
> Christ, in our fear of being seen as we are, we
> discover all too late that it's impossible to be
> fully human and fully alive.[1]
>
> We have nothing of any value to lose by being real; indeed,
> we have all of God's best to gain.

C. Sovereignty. This is the third attribute Christ ascribed to Himself. It means that He has control over all things. The keys to life
and death, heaven and hell, and even ministry are in His grasp
(compare Isaiah 22:15–22, Acts 16:6–10, Rev. 1:18). He opens and
closes doors at His discretion. No one can shut what He has
opened or pry loose what He has closed. How foolish we are
when we try to knock down barriers He has set up or fail to walk
down paths He has cleared! We miss so much good when we attempt to go our own way.

II. The Church Commended
In Revelation 3:8, Jesus turns to give the Philadelphian church three
compliments.
A. Little power—big potential. The Philadelphian assembly
was not great in size or influence; she was "small potatoes" compared to other churches. But Christ saw that her little bit of power
had tremendous potential. For that He commended her.
B. Biblical fidelity. Christ also praised the church for keeping
to His Word. Unlike the congregation at Sardis (v. 3), she not
only knew the truth but practiced it as well.
C. Good reputation. The believers in Philadelphia were also
applauded for not buckling under persecution. They stood strong
for Christ, refusing to deny their faith.

III. The Church Rewarded
Because of the church's faithfulness to the Lord, she was given a
great opportunity for ministry (v. 8): evangelistic outreach to the

1. Tim Hansel, *When I Relax I Feel Guilty* (Elgin, Ill.: David C. Cook Publishing Co., 1979), p. 87.

neighboring country we know today as Turkey. Geographically, Philadelphia was located in a strategic spot—"at the juncture of trade routes leading to Mysia, Lydia, and Phrygia."[2] Consequently, Philadelphia was known as the gateway to the East. It was such an influential city that it was used by imperial authorities to spread the Greek culture and language to Lydia and Phrygia. Philadelphia was highly successful in this task, evidenced by the fact that before A.D. 19 "the Lydian tongue had been replaced by Greek as the only language of the country."[3] Now, however, the Authority over all authorities had chosen the tiny church in Philadelphia to reach Turkey with His gospel. He had opened the door; all the Philadelphian Christians had to do was walk through it.

IV. The Lord's Promises
Christ knew, however, that this new opportunity would bring increased opposition. Flies, like enemies, tend to take advantage of open doors, moving through them, leaving their germs on everything they touch. But Jesus encouraged the Philadelphian church not to worry about the flies. Let's look at the ways He promised to protect her and give her victory over her enemies.

A. "I will humiliate your enemies." Notice how Jesus put it: " 'Behold, I will cause those of the synagogue of Satan, who say that they are Jews, and are not, but lie—behold, I will make them to come and bow down at your feet, and to know that I have loved you' " (v. 9). True Jews—completed Jews—are descendants of Abraham and have found forgiveness and new life in Jesus the Messiah (see Rom. 2:28–29, Phil. 3:3–11). Deceiving Jews are those who reject and persecute believers in Christ. Consequently, they are children of Satan, the demonic accuser of Christians (see John 8:39–41, 44; Rev. 12:7–10; compare 2 Cor. 11:14–15). Jesus promised the Philadelphian church that He would humble her enemies and make them acknowledge what they refused to accept—that the church is the object of the Messiah's love. Christ did not say when this promise would be fulfilled, but He did assure the church that He would accomplish it. We do know that someday all opposers of Christ will kneel at His feet and confess that He is Lord (Phil. 2:9–11). His enemies may not pay daily for their sin . . . but one day payment in full will be required. This should give us courage to press on without seeking revenge (see Rom. 12:19–21).

2. Robert H. Mounce, *The Book of Revelation* (Grand Rapids, Mich.: William B. Eerdmans Publishing Co., 1977), p. 114.

3. Mounce, *The Book of Revelation,* p. 115.

B. "I will keep you from maximum affliction." The second promise, found in Revelation 3:10, assures Christ's people that He will keep them " 'from the hour of testing, that hour which is about to come upon the whole world, to test those who dwell upon the earth.' " The "hour of testing" is known as the Tribulation—a seven-year period of intense, devastating divine judgment that will affect the entire earth (see Rev. 6–19). Christ promised the Philadelphian believers—as He promises all others who trust in Him—that He would protect them from this awful expression of God's wrath. In this context, the Greek phrase translated *keep from* does not mean "to preserve through something" but "to preserve outside the sphere of something." Jesus is saying that He will protect believers from the Tribulation by keeping them away from it. In fact, He will remove them from the earth before the seven-year judgment begins.[4] Our faith may encounter heavy opposition; we may even suffer persecution because we're Christians. But at no time will we experience the great affliction the Tribulation will bring upon those unbelievers unfortunate enough to still be alive.

C. "I will make you strong and secure." The Lord said that He would make the Philadelphian church—a church of little power—into a pillar of strength (3:12a). No matter what verbal, psychological, or physical abuse would come her way, she would be able to withstand it because her foundation would be God Himself. As Christians, we have the same security and strength available to us. So great is our power through Him "that neither death, nor life, nor angels, nor principalities, nor things present, nor things to come, nor powers, nor height, nor depth, nor any other created thing, [can] separate us from the love of God, which is in Christ Jesus our Lord" (Rom. 8:38–39).

D. "I will give you a new identity." Christ's fourth promise concerned the reputation of the church at Philadelphia. He assured them that He would make their good name even better. How? By giving them the name of His heavenly Father (Rev. 3:12b), something that was already occurring by the transforming work of the Holy Spirit. He was conforming them into Christ's perfect image by making them godly in mind, will, and conduct. But the process would not be complete until they stood totally blameless before God's throne (1 Thess. 5:23–24, Jude 24, Rev. 14:1–5). We who are Christians are also under construction. One day, we will be perfectly restored reflectors of Christ, made worthy to receive the name of our holy Father. In the meantime, we need

4. This interpretation is substantiated by Jeffrey L. Townsend in his article "The Rapture in Revelation 3:10," *Bibliotheca Sacra* 137 (July–September 1980), pp. 252–66.

to surrender ourselves to the work of God's Spirit, cooperating with His efforts to make us like Jesus (see Rom. 12:1–2, Eph. 5:18, Col. 3:9–11).

V. Some Final Thoughts

The Philadelphian church was definitely a model body of believers. We have already learned a great deal from them, but before we move on, there are two more observations we can make that are worth pondering.

A. Immeasurable opportunities turn our attention back to God. Open doors are great, but the tremendous responsibilities they present quickly show us our utter inadequacy—and His infinite sufficiency.

B. Immeasurable opportunities take the sting out of affliction. With open doors come the flies of opposition. But as long as our focus is on Christ, our Protector and Sustainer, we'll be able to face and even overcome the struggles that come our way.

 Living Insights

Study One

First-century Philadelphia was quite different from today's home of the Phillies. It was a small city, but it housed a church rich in opportunity.

- So far, we've looked at six of the seven churches. Let's use this study to compare and contrast two of the churches. Use the church at Philadelphia as one and choose another one you are interested in. Copy the following chart and jot down the similarities and differences you discover as you reread the letters to the two churches.

Two Churches: Philadelphia and _____	
Similarities	Differences

Living Insights

The Lord used an effective communication method by writing letters to the seven churches. Let's hitchhike on the same technique as we personalize what we've learned.

- Can you imagine what God would say in a letter to you? Take some time and write it out, just as you think He would say it.
- Now, respond to His letter with your own reply. Answer any questions that were raised. Discuss your feelings openly. Talk to Him about your strengths and weaknesses, as well as your plans to act on His comments.

Our Number One Spiritual Battle
Revelation 3:14–19

The writer Joaquim Maria Machado de Assis tells the story of a well-to-do woman living with her family and an aspiring college student. It's a story of tolerance taken to an extreme. Intimately involved with another woman, her husband spent the night with his mistress once every week. The wife knew about her mate's rendezvous but never tried to stop him. Though his affair grieved her at first, she eventually became "used to the situation . . . , and finally she came almost to accept the affair as proper."[1] The young student living with the family described her as a person with "a temperament of great equanimity, with extremes neither of tears nor of laughter. Everything about her was passive. . . . She was what is called a kind person. She spoke ill of no one, she pardoned everything. She didn't know how to hate; quite possibly she didn't know how to love."[2] Indifference replaced zeal; approval supplanted sorrow; tolerance suppressed truth. In a similar progression, the first-century church of Laodicea allowed her devotion to Christ to shift into neutral. She no longer wrestled with evil or defended the faith—instead, she tolerated everything, neither loving nor hating anything. Christ attacked her spiritual blandness with some of the harshest words found anywhere in Scripture. Let's examine the letter He sent to this church and see what it has to say to us.

I. The Case of the Laodicean Church

Before delving into the letter, let's get an overview of the city of Laodicea and its church.

A. The city. Located about 145 miles southeast of Philadelphia and about 100 miles east of Ephesus, Laodicea sat in the fertile lap of the Lycus Valley. As an important center of trade and communication, Laodicea prospered, partly through "the production of a fine quality of famous glossy black wool."[3] Her wealth was so great that after the devastating earthquake of A.D. 17, "the people refused imperial help in rebuilding the city, choosing rather to do it entirely by themselves."[4] Besides the city's abundant riches, "there were no excesses or notable achievements to distinguish it. It was a city with a people who had learned to

1. See Joaquim Maria Machado de Assis, "Midnight Mass," in *Short Fiction of the Masters,* ed. Leo Hamalian and Frederick R. Karl (New York, N.Y.: G. P. Putnam's Sons, 1963), p. 84.

2. Machado de Assis, "Midnight Mass," p. 84.

3. Alan Johnson, "Revelation," in *The Expositor's Bible Commentary* (Grand Rapids, Mich.: Regency Reference Library, Zondervan Publishing House, 1981), vol. 12, p. 456.

4. Johnson, "Revelation," p. 456.

compromise and accommodate themselves to the needs and wishes of others.... They did not zealously stand for anything."[5]

B. The church. The first converts in Laodicea probably came to Christ as a result of the ministries of Paul and Epaphras (Acts 19:8–10, Col. 4:12–13). The letter to the Colossian Christians, which was also to be sent to the Laodicean church, reveals Paul's concern for the pastor in Laodicea and may hint at the fact that he was losing his passion for ministry (Col. 4:16–17). Generally speaking, the condition of the shepherd mirrors the state of his flock. If the primary leader of the Laodicean church was cooling down, chances are good that the church was as well. She was in the process of yawning herself into spiritual indifference.

II. The Divine Investigator

Toward the end of the first century, the Laodicean church received a letter of assessment from Jesus Christ. In it, He identified Himself before highlighting the congregation's main problem. First, He described Himself as " 'the Amen' " (Rev. 3:14), emphasizing the certainty and validity of His words. Second, He called Himself " 'the faithful and true Witness' " (v. 14a)—consistent and reliable. And third, He said He was " 'the Beginning of the creation of God' " (v. 14b)—the creative Source of the entire universe (see John 1:1–3). As we will see, the church in Laodicea needed to be reminded of these truths.

III. The Lord's Findings and Reactions

Revelation 3:15–17 exposes the condition of the Laodicean church and Christ's response to it. The description is vivid and His reaction stern. This passage will alert us to what provokes the Lord's anger so we can avoid it at all costs.

A. The condition of the church. Christ said, " 'I know your deeds, that you are neither cold nor hot.... You are lukewarm' " (vv. 15–16a). The church was like Laodicea's drinking water— lukewarm and flat. Laodicea's water was so unsavory that visitors often vomited after drinking it[6]... and so it was with the church. She wasn't cold or lifeless; on the contrary, she was filled with believers who were positive additions to the community, who blended in and became respectable, peaceable members of society. But the church wasn't hot or zealous, either. Undoubtedly, the Laodicean believers used Christian lingo, smiled at children, occasionally gave of their finances, and discussed the needs of their community. But did they selflessly give of themselves? Did

5. Johnson, "Revelation," p. 456.

6. See "Revelation," by Johnson, p. 457, and *The Book of Revelation*, by Robert H. Mounce (Grand Rapids, Mich.: William B. Eerdmans Publishing Co., 1977), p. 125.

they stand up for Christ—courageously sharing the gospel, defending the faith, ministering to the needy, and fighting injustice? Hardly. They did what many Christians do today: they sat, soaked, and soured. Content with material prosperity and social acceptance, they grew indifferent to biblical truth and its application. In other words, they lost the number one spiritual battle Christians face: the fight against compromise and complacency. And they didn't even realize how bad off they had become. As Jesus described them, " 'You say, "I am rich, and have become wealthy, and have need of nothing," and you do not know that you are wretched and miserable and poor and blind and naked' " (v. 17). In contrast to Christ, their words and works were a sham. They were spiritually unfaithful, unreliable, and destructive. They were nauseatingly tepid, and they didn't even know it.

B. The response of Christ. The Lord reacted to the church's condition with condemnation. Christ told her He would prefer that she were cold or hot—apostate or loyal—rather than lukewarm. Why? Because the most difficult people to deal with are bland, blind religionists. Little ruffles their feathers or moves them off the fence of compromise. Conformity at any price is the name of their game. Talk to them about involvement in an unpopular social cause, missions to the world's lost, or the discipleship of new Christians, and you'll probably get kind comments of agreement but no solid actions of commitment. No wonder Christ said He was ready to vomit the Laodiceans out of His mouth (v. 16)! Their complacency rendered them useless to Him; their empty religiosity made Him sick.

IV. Christ's Solution

Although the Lord was disgusted with the Laodicean Christians, He was not about to give up on them. With patience, grace, and a firm hand, He offered these believers a cure for their disease—a remedy available to all of us who suffer from lukewarm faith.

A. Exchange wretched poverty for pure gold. Spiritual apathy cannot be cured by material prosperity. Like the Laodiceans, we need to receive spiritual wealth from Christ by serving Him faithfully (v. 18a; compare Matt. 6:19–21, Rom. 12:1–2). Among other things, this involves a willingness to commit ourselves and our resources to His work in our local churches, surrounding communities, and overseas nations. Do you make yourself that available?

B. Exchange stark nakedness for white garments. All too often, we strut in front of others thinking we are clothed with commitment to Christ, when in reality we are as naked as the emperor in his invisible clothes. The Laodiceans were like this,

46

only they didn't need the sleek, black wool of their city—they needed to be clothed with the virgin white garments of forgiveness only Christ could supply (Rev. 3:18b). How can this clothing be obtained? By a personal act of confession and rededication to the Lord. There is no other way. Are you willing to pay this price?

C. Exchange destructive blindness for healing eye-salve. When our ability to honestly evaluate ourselves becomes so impaired that we can't see the personal effects of spiritual compromise and mediocrity, we need the sight-restoring balm that's available through Christ (v. 18). No modern medicine is useful in curing cases of self-deception. Would you ask the Lord to restore your perspective so you might view yourself as He does?

D. Exchange lukewarm indifference for hot zealousness. Our decisions must be accompanied with appropriate actions in order to bring about genuine change. When we fall short in applying truth, we risk coming under the correcting hand of Christ (v. 19a). Are you prepared to live for Him rather than merely thinking and talking about Him?

E. Exchange compromising disobedience for true repentance. Spiritual fires cannot be rekindled without the fresh fuel of a changed mind and will (v. 19b). Are you ready to get serious about Christ—to start ordering your private and public worlds according to His written Word?

V. Our Response

Let's become even more specific in our application of the Laodicean letter. Let's concentrate on missions, seeking to combat personal fence straddling by reviewing and renewing our commitment to God's worldwide outreach to the lost. Thoughtfully consider the following five statements. After deciding which ones you would like to pursue, outline and begin implementing a realistic course of action. Be sure to bathe this whole process in prayer, placing Christ at the center with His resources at your disposal.

A. I plan to dedicate the rest of my life to missionary work.

B. I plan to give one or more short periods of my life to missionary work.

C. I plan to pray regularly for specific missionary concerns.

D. I plan to participate in my church's missionary program.

E. I plan to develop a close friendship with an international student.

Continued on next page

Living Insights

Study One ▬▬▬▬▬▬▬▬▬▬▬▬▬▬▬▬▬▬▬▬▬

Laodicea = Lukewarm. The church was neither cold nor hot. And, tragically, many of us know of modern-day Laodicean churches ... and people.

• Do you know other biblical churches or characters that could be characterized by the term "lukewarm"? How about "hot"? "Cold"? Copy the following charts and find five biblical examples for each of the three categories.

Lukewarm	References	Reasons
1.		
2.		
3.		
4.		
5.		

Hot	References	Reasons
1.		
2.		
3.		
4.		
5.		

Cold	References	Reasons
1.		
2.		
3.		
4.		
5.		

 Living Insights

Study Two ▬▬▬▬▬▬▬▬▬▬▬▬▬▬▬▬▬▬▬▬▬

The church in Laodicea left a bad taste in God's mouth—how would He feel about *your* life?

- Instead of lukewarm, hot, and cold, use a different measurement to evaluate your own life. If you were a car, what gear would best characterize your Christian life? Circle one; then write down the reasons for your choice.

P	R	N	D

- Are you satisfied in your present gear? How can you move into a higher gear? Spend ten minutes thinking through a plan for improvement.
- Let's talk with God. Openly share with Him your thoughts and feelings. Talk about your plan and ask Him for the strength to follow through.

The Case of the Excluded King
Revelation 3:20–22

Let your mind wander back to the days of nobles, princes, queens, and kings. Imagine a medieval castle with huge cylindrical towers and immaculately kept courtyards. Servants are busy tending to the needs of the nobility. Jesters are practicing new acts; musicians are rehearsing for the evening's banquet. Observing people's activities and overhearing their conversations, you soon come to realize that everything is revolving around one man—the king. Entering a spacious, high-ceilinged room through massive arched doors, your eyes fall on a tall, bearded man, finely dressed and stately in manner. He appears to be a gentle, fun-loving man; his subjects obey because of his beneficence and high rank rather than intimidation. A courier approaches him with news of a rebellion in the land. Contrary to your expectations, however, the king does not order his knights and infantry to squelch the resistance. Instead, he changes into peasant clothes, leaves the castle alone, and journeys on foot to the makeshift headquarters of the rebels. Once there, he slips past the guards and steps up to the entrance of the small house-turned-command center. He knocks on the door, identifies himself, and offers the rebels a complete pardon if they will let him in and lay down their arms. He even promises that in exchange for their surrender, he will treat them as his closest friends and give them authority to rule the land with him. Sound like a fairy tale? On a purely human level, it is. But from the divine perspective, this story depicts the condescension of the heavenly King to the rebellious planet Earth. Putting aside His radiant royal glory, He took on the humble clothing of human flesh and walked among His enemies, holding out the promise of complete forgiveness and corulership with Him if they would surrender to Him by faith. Today, the King is not among us physically, but as we'll see, He is still present, and His offer remains the same.

I. A Review of the Seven Churches

We've covered a lot of territory in this series, so before we begin to bring it to a close, let's review where we've been. Jesus Christ, the Creator and sovereign King, dictated seven letters to the pastors of seven churches who were to read the royal mail to their congregations. In each letter, Christ addressed a danger that Christians have faced for centuries.

A. Ephesus—the danger of diminishing love. Though doctrinally sound and faithfully persistent, the Ephesian believers had lost their deep devotion to Christ. They needed to rekindle the flame that once burned so warmly for the Savior.

B. Smyrna—the danger of fearing suffering. The Christians in Smyrna were under intense persecution and were confronting the likelihood of even greater adversity. Consequently, they needed to be encouraged to stand firm for the Lord rather than deny Him out of fear for their lives.

C. Pergamum—the danger of doctrinal compromise. Because of tolerating heresy among some of her members, the church in Pergamum was beginning to drift from her biblical moorings. In order to return to the harbor of truth, she was told to stop compromising. Otherwise, punishment would follow.

D. Thyatira—the danger of moral compromise. With a Jezebel in the congregation, many believers in Thyatira were led into condoning and committing sin. They needed to turn their lives back to Christ and make His standard of purity their own.

E. Sardis—the danger of spiritual deadness. The assembly at Sardis was a morgue with a steeple. Though she had a reputation of being religiously vibrant, she was actually dead in her devotion to Christ. What she lacked Christ offered to give—new life and restored usefulness.

F. Philadelphia—the danger of failing to advance. The Philadelphian Christians were small in number but large in potential. They were capable of carrying the good news of salvation far beyond their immediate community. So Jesus opened the door of evangelistic opportunity and encouraged them to walk through it with His power and protection.

G. Laodicea—the danger of indifference. Self-sufficiency and self-satisfaction blinded the believers of Laodicea to their desperate spiritual condition. Christ, however, exposed their problem: apathy to godly matters. Sickened by their lukewarm state, the Lord called on them to turn back to Him before He had to resort to discipline.

II. An Exposition of the Last Three Verses

Our study brings us to the final verses of the last letter. Granted, Revelation 3:20–22 is attached to the letter intended for the Laodicean congregation. But in many respects, these verses are a fitting close to all of the letters. Indeed, their message penetrates to the heart of the Christian gospel, making their practical import universal in scope. We'll seek to understand these verses by addressing six questions—each answered clearly in the text itself.

A. Who is speaking? The verses are spoken in the first person, as are the several verses that precede them. We know that the speaker in chapters 2 and 3 is Christ—the Son of God and King of Kings (Rev. 1:1–2, 17–18; 2:27). Therefore, the One who is standing at the door and knocking in chapter 3, verse 20, must be Christ.

B. What does the door represent? Some expositors think the door symbolizes the future kingdom of Christ—the one He will establish on earth when He comes back to rule after the Tribulation. Support for this interpretation frequently comes from parallel passages that depict the Lord standing at the door of judgment, ready to enter and deal out retribution (Mark 13:28–29, James 5:8–9). There are two problems with this view. First, in these passages on judgment, the Greek term for *door* is plural, whereas it is singular in Revelation 3:20. This difference in number likely indicates that the door in Revelation 3 stands for an idea other than judgment. Second, when Christ comes to judge the nations, He will burst on the scene as a fearsome commander, leading the heavenly armies in righteous warfare (19:11–21). This is a much different picture of Christ than the one given in Revelation 3. There He stands at the door and knocks, patiently waiting for an invitation to enter. Therefore, it seems more likely that this door represents the entrance into a person's life. Jesus is saying, "Look, I'm here in your presence, desiring to become the center of your life. Will you open your heart to Me?"

C. How does He seek entrance? Jesus will not batter down a door, forcing His way into someone's life. Instead, He waits outside and knocks, making His presence known but waiting for an invitation to enter. As He says, " 'I stand at the door and knock; if anyone hears My voice and opens the door, I will come into Him' " (v. 20). But how does He make Himself known? He taps us on the shoulder and speaks to our souls. He peers through the windows of our lives, exposing our need for Him to enter the library of our minds, the living room of our wills, and the kitchen of our conduct. Nothing is left uncovered, not even our deepest emotions or most private thoughts. Proverbs 20:27 makes this clear: "The spirit of man is the lamp of the Lord, / Searching all the innermost parts of his being."

D. To whom is the appeal made? Jesus says, " 'If *anyone* hears My voice . . .' " (Rev. 3:20, emphasis added). His offer is universal. He stands on the doorstep of every life, making His presence known and asking entrance.

A Personal Request

Jesus is not like the marines, looking for a few good men who have the mettle to be loyal Christians. He's the King of the universe, standing at the door of every rebel heart, offering Himself and His abundant resources to rebuild shattered lives and mend broken hearts. He's speaking to you. If you're not a Christian, He is asking to enter your life, remove your guilt, and reconcile you to God. If you have already accepted Christ by faith, His request is that

---

you allow Him to enter more rooms of your life. Perhaps He's still an outsider in your business. Or maybe you have excluded Him from your home, recreation time, or education. Whatever the case, He has more to give you if you'll simply grant His request to come in. Will you do that? Will you do it today—even right now?

E. **What response does He desire?** The excluded King seeks a response of open acceptance (v. 20). We can open the door by believing He is our King and trusting in His Word (John 3:16, Rom. 10:8–13).

F. **What happens when the door is opened?** " 'I will come into him, and will dine with him, and he with Me' " (Rev. 3:20b). The Greek term Christ uses for *dine* refers to the main meal of the day. During the first century, this was the evening meal. It wasn't eaten on the run; this mealtime was set aside for relaxation, enjoyment, and fellowship. Invitations to share this meal were usually offered to close friends. Christ alludes to this time of relational intimacy to show that we who open our lives to Him will commune with Him as with a loved one or bosom friend. He will fill our lives with His comforting presence and loving counsel. Then when He returns to earth to establish His kingdom, He will invite us to sit with Him on His throne and rule with Him over the nations of the world (v. 21; see Luke 22:29–30, Rev. 20:4).

III. **Responses to Two Final Promises**

Jesus promised that if we open ourselves to Him, He will enter our lives and fellowship with us. If you have invited Him in, thank Him for His intimate presence in your life, and express gratitude for the nourishment He has given you. Remember, He left His heavenly throne to save us from self-destruction. And He did this even when we were rebelling against Him, totally undeserving of His love and compassion. How caring He has been! How grateful we should be.

 Living Insights

Study One ▬▬▬▬▬▬▬▬▬▬▬▬▬▬▬▬▬▬▬▬▬▬▬▬▬▬▬

We began this series with an overview of the seven churches, expressing initial impressions of each of the seven letters. Let's go back to those now and do some reflecting.

- Look back at your chart from the first lesson. Do you still see the seven churches the same way you did then? What changes have

Continued on next page

taken place in your thinking? Copy the chart below and make a summary statement about each church; then see how they compare with your first impressions.

Churches	Verses	Summary Statements
Ephesus	2:1–7	
Smyrna	2:8–11	
Pergamum	2:12–17	
Thyatira	2:18–29	
Sardis	3:1–6	
Philadelphia	3:7–13	
Laodicea	3:14–19	

 Living Insights

Study Two ▬▬▬▬▬▬▬▬▬▬▬▬▬▬▬▬▬▬▬▬▬▬

You'll also recall that in the first lesson we charted some appropriate applications for our lives. How did that work out? Do you feel your life is changed in some way as a result of this study?

• This time as you copy the chart, write down the applications that are most meaningful to you. The purpose of Bible study is application, so let's review to see what life-changing principles God brought to your mind.

Will You Lead or Lag?

1 Corinthians 14, Exodus 18

Have you noticed that things aren't always as they appear? Take icebergs, for example. The peak of ice protruding above the surface is nothing compared to the enormous frozen mountain below the waterline. In fact, only one-eighth to one-tenth of an iceberg's total mass is visible above the water. Another instance of appearance differing from reality is found in the local church. Like icebergs, churches have a few highly noticeable leaders, which tends to give the impression that the visible few run the entire ministry. But nothing could be further from the truth. With rare exceptions, churches have small pastoral staffs that are aided by a comparatively large number of laypeople. These unpaid volunteers serve in the nursery, teach Sunday school, answer telephones, sing in the choir, and help care for bedridden church members. Whatever their task, little ministry could occur without them. And yet, their service is rarely, if ever, seen by the public. They are the ones below the waterline, invisibly affecting the total development of the congregation they serve. At any rate, one thing is certain: Churches need competent people who can lead in visible, high-profile positions. But they also need qualified people who can serve without a ripple, below the surface. Without both groups cooperating, the ministry will struggle to stay afloat, if not sink altogether.

I. The Godliness of Management

Organization requires orderliness; the two go hand-in-hand. Therefore, a church that lacks one lacks the other. And when neither is present, leadership is impossible. Some people argue that the Lord desires creativity and spontaneity, both of which are squelched by a structured atmosphere. The truth is that God wants ingenuity, but He wants it expressed within the bounds of good management. First Corinthians 14 demonstrates this clearly.

A. Disorder is out. The Corinthian church was a body out of balance. Her members were divisive, prideful, and immature. And although these infamous traits revealed themselves in a number of ways, one of the most disturbing was in their manner of worship. People were exercising their spiritual gifts when and how they wanted, without bearing in mind what would benefit the whole congregation. As a result, mayhem rather than edification was becoming the visible mark of the church (vv. 9–12, 16–24, 26). The Apostle Paul sought to put an end to this by reminding the Corinthians of a crucial truth: "God is not a God of confusion" (v. 33a). According to New Testament scholar W. Harold Mare, the Greek term translated *confusion* "is a strong one, indicating great disturbance, disorder, or even insurrection or revolution (Luke 21:9)."[1] In other words, disorder violates God's character—therefore, He doesn't want it to characterize His people, especially when they gather to worship Him. Likewise, He is not pleased by poor management. Ministries that are haphazardly run misrepresent the Lord they claim to serve.

B. Order is in. Far from representing confusion, God is instead the God of peace (v. 33a). His nature is perfect and unified; the persons of the Godhead always act in harmony. Hence, He wants His people to do "all things . . . properly and in an orderly manner" (v. 40). And this, of course, includes the management of local churches. Do well-organized ministries stifle creativity? Perhaps some do, but not out of necessity. Indeed, a church marked by peace actually gives her members the freedom they need to use their gifts most effectively for Christian service (see 12:4–25, 14:26–31).

II. Four Laws of Leadership

The key to good church management is godly people leading the congregation according to biblical principles. This truth is illustrated throughout Scripture, but one of the most revealing instances is found in Exodus 18. The leader is Moses. His congregation consists of more than two million members,[2] and he is shepherding them in the barren, mountainous terrain of the southern end of the Sinai Peninsula. His father-in-law Jethro, his wife, and two sons go out to meet him. When Jethro sees Moses playing the role of sole administrator of God's laws, he asks Moses, " 'What is this thing that you are doing for the people? Why do you alone sit as judge and all the people stand about you from morning until evening?' " (v. 14). Jethro confronts Moses' single-handed leadership with four timeless principles for godly leadership.

A. One person, no matter how gifted, cannot do a big job alone. Jethro tells Moses, " 'The thing that you are doing is not good. You will surely wear out, both yourself and these people who are with you, for the task is too heavy for you; you cannot do it alone' " (vv. 17–18). Jethro was right. His son-in-law was trying to meet the needs of more people than he could possibly handle. Consequently, he was headed toward burnout, and the people were becoming frustrated with all the delays. Regardless of his good intentions, Moses had to stop playing the role of a lone ranger—the nature and size of his task demanded that he adopt a more suitable management approach. If your emotions

1. W. Harold Mare, "1 Corinthians," in *The Expositor's Bible Commentary* (Grand Rapids, Mich.: Regency Reference Library, Zondervan Publishing Co., 1976), vol. 10, p. 276.

2. See John J. Davis's *Moses and the Gods of Egypt: Studies in the Book of Exodus* (Grand Rapids, Mich.: Baker Book House, 1971), p. 146.

are wearing thin and the job has become drudgery, you are probably trying to tackle too much on your own. Be advised: don't keep it up! In the long run, it will only hurt you and those you serve.

B. **High-visibility leadership is needed, but its role must be limited.** Jethro continues, " 'Now listen to me: I shall give you counsel, and God be with you. You be the people's representative before God, and you bring the disputes to God, then teach them the statutes and the laws, and make known to them the way in which they are to walk, and the work they are to do' " (vv. 19–20). Jethro didn't think Moses should fade into the background or walk away from his primary responsibilities. Rather, he encouraged his son-in-law to maintain a highly visible leadership role, adding to it some built-in restrictions. His advice was right on target. Leaders cannot have direct contact with everything that goes on in their ministries without spreading themselves too thin. They should inform, guide, and encourage their followers, not attempt to perform every task themselves.

C. **Big loads should be borne by many people, but these individuals must be selected carefully.** Jethro applies this principle in his counsel to Moses:

> "You shall select out of all the people able men who
> fear God, men of truth, those who hate dishonest gain;
> and you shall place these over them, as leaders....
> And let them judge the people at all times; and let it
> be that every major dispute they will bring to you,
> but every minor dispute they themselves will judge.
> So it will be easier for you, and they will bear the bur-
> den with you." (vv. 21–22)

Many congregations today assume that their leaders are not doing their jobs unless they look physically and emotionally drained. God contradicts this perspective, stating through Jethro that a leader's role is to become lighter, not heavier, as qualified people are found to help share the load. And what are the requisite qualifications? Those who serve God's people are to have the necessary skills for the task. They are to fear God, to possess integrity, to disdain dishonesty. They should not be selected by chance, because they have always performed the job, have seniority, or happen to be related to influential church members. The Lord wants people with the right skills and proven character to carry on the tasks of ministry. When individuals like these are in place, the work can get done in an effective, orderly way. Also, church leaders, especially the more visible ones, can secure the time they need to develop and exercise their particular gifts for the edification of the church body. If you have been chosen to serve, whether in the spotlight or behind the scenes, be sure to carry your part of the load so someone else doesn't end up shouldering a double share.

D. When there is proper management, leaders don't wear out and harmony prevails. Notice how Jethro conveys this truth: " 'If you do this thing and God so commands you, then you will be able to endure, and all these people also will go to their place in peace' " (v. 23). Burnout, frustration, confusion— these are telltale signs of poor management. On the other hand, an organized team can be recognized by its fruits of cooperation, understanding, support, cheerfulness, and the satisfaction of a job well done.

III. Two Marks of a Good Leader

Moses manifests leadership ability in two ways. First, he listens to the advice of his father-in-law (v. 24a). It takes humility to consider criticism without getting upset or pulling rank. Moses was willing to hear Jethro speak his mind, thereby taking the first step toward needed change. Second, Moses sets Jethro's plan in motion, and it works out just as he said it would (vv. 24b–26). Everyone benefits when leaders are wise enough to implement sound advice. Moses understood this and acted accordingly.

IV. Three Thoughts to Ponder

As we bring this study to a close, let's give our attention to some final thoughts that are pertinent to all of us involved in a local church.

A. Selecting leaders is serious business; we dare not take it lightly. We need to take whatever steps are necessary to ensure that the best people are chosen for the right jobs. And this involves a consideration of character . . . of willingness to be part of a team . . . and of pure motives for wanting to lead.

B. Those who become leaders automatically become models. It's a fact: congregations reflect the strengths and weaknesses of their leaders. This is one more reason for choosing truly qualified people to lead—individuals who manifest the traits that your churches should model.

C. We must be willing to follow those we appoint to lead us. Hebrews 13:17 says it well: "Obey your leaders, and submit to them; for they keep watch over your soul, as those who will give an account [to God]. Let them do this with joy and not with grief, for this would be unprofitable for you." Our church leaders need our cooperation if we're to benefit from their service. Are you a supportive follower? If not, you may be missing out on some blessings God would like to give you.

Living Insights

We took a brief look at the leadership style of Moses shown in Exodus 18. Both the Old and New Testaments abound with examples of proper leadership. Let's take a close-up look at another leader.

● Take some time to skim through Nehemiah 1–8. As you read, make mental notes of the leadership qualities demonstrated by this man. Then copy the chart below into your notebook and fill in the traits of good leadership you noticed, along with corresponding Scripture references.

Nehemiah the Leader	
References	Leadership Qualities

 Living Insights

Based on what we've seen in the lives of Moses and Nehemiah, let's check out our own leadership leanings. The results may be quite revealing.

● Looking over your chart from Study One, do you see leadership characteristics in Nehemiah that you possess as well? Jot them down.
● Every leader is an individual. You have certain leadership capabilities unique to you. Write down some of the reasons you are special in the arena of leaders.
● Wrap this time up with prayer. Maybe you've been involved in areas that don't really parallel your strengths. Perhaps you have leanings toward areas in which you're not involved. Ask God for direction and guidance. Request Him to show you the *right* context for your leadership strengths.

Books for Probing Further

As football players know, the best offense is a good defense. In order to win, they need to prepare, prepare, and prepare some more. Their training involves physical conditioning, learning plays, dealing with opposition, and following the coach's game plan. Victory in the Christian life is obtained in much the same way. Believers need to mature in their walk with God, understand how to face opposition, and be submissive to human authority. Realizing these truths, we have assembled a list of books that can help you triumph in the Christian life. We trust you will use these resources as supplements, not as substitutes, to your study and application of God's Word.

I. Knowing the King

Packer, J. I. *Knowing God.* Downers Grove, Ill.: InterVarsity Press, 1973. The most practical, life-changing project we can engage in is coming to know God as fully as possible. This book certainly doesn't exhaust the subject, but it does ignite the heart to continue the quest until it ends in heavenly bliss.

Sproul, R. C. *The Holiness of God.* Wheaton, Ill.: Tyndale House Publishers, 1985. God calls us to be holy as He is holy, but we cannot fully obey this command until we *understand* His holiness. Through a challenging and richly rewarding exploration of Scripture and church history, Sproul sheds light on God's perfect character and clarifies how we can manifest it in our lives.

II. Obeying the King

Colson, Charles W. *Loving God.* Grand Rapids, Mich.: Zondervan Publishing House, 1983. The first step to obeying God is realizing that He demonstrated His love for us when we were unworthy to receive it. Colson powerfully illuminates this truth in what has become a classic. He will move you not only to awe and thankfulness for the Lord's love but to a life dedicated to loving Him in return.

MacDonald, Gordon. *Ordering Your Private World.* Chicago, Ill.: Moody Press, 1984. As we learned in our study, God is a God of order, not confusion. He wants us to organize our lives according to the principles and commands of His Word. This process must begin in our inner lives—our private worlds. MacDonald shows you how to realign your inner world so you can live at peace in an often chaotic outer world.

Swindoll, Charles R. *Strengthening Your Grip: Essentials in an Aimless World.* Waco, Tex.: Word Books, 1982. Would you like to know how to keep your priorities straight, maintain integrity, grow in the faith, pray more effectively, and cherish family life? With realism and practicality, Swindoll tackles these issues and many more in this fresh look at the Christian life.

III. Suffering under the King

Strauss, Lehman. *In God's Waiting Room: Learning Through Suffering.* Chicago, Ill.: Moody Press, 1985. Christians suffer like anyone else. However, unlike unbelievers, Christians have divine resources available to them that can help see them through even the darkest days. This book makes plain the assets we have, giving us a greater ability to cope with and even appreciate our pain.

Swindoll, Charles R. *Encourage Me.* Portland, Oreg.: Multnomah Press, 1982. When the believers in Smyrna were being persecuted, Christ reached out and encouraged them. You may not be experiencing affliction because of your faith, but you may be hurting nonetheless, wishing—perhaps silently—that someone would uplift your soul. This book does just that, opening up the truths of Scripture and allowing God to restore your strength and perspective.

IV. Serving the King's Subjects

Peterson, Eugene H. *Five Smooth Stones for Pastoral Work.* Atlanta, Ga.: John Knox Press, 1980. Drawing from five Old Testament books and more than twenty years of pastoral experience, the author presents timeless principles of ministry for vocational Christian workers and laypeople alike. This book is rich in theological and practical insight.

Sanders, J. Oswald. *Spiritual Leadership.* Revised edition. Chicago, Ill.: Moody Press, 1980. Perhaps never before in history has the Church needed talented, vigorous leaders as she does today. And yet, there seems to be a dearth of good leaders and great confusion over what constitutes good leadership. Sanders cuts through the fog, presenting a clear biblical picture of godly leadership.

Swindoll, Charles R. *Improving Your Serve: The Art of Unselfish Living.* Waco, Tex.: Word Books, 1981. The heart of spiritual leadership and the Christian life is the art of serving. We cannot help others or ourselves as we should until we learn how to give without always expecting to receive. Swindoll shows us how to move away from a lifestyle of selfishness toward one marked by unselfish service.

Insight for Living
Cassette Tapes
LETTERS TO CHURCHES ... THEN AND NOW

Unlike the more familiar letters from the New Testament, these are tucked away in the early chapters of Revelation. And yet they are as practical and helpful as anything written by Paul, Peter, or James. Seven letters to churches that existed in the first century ... but you'll think they were written to the church you attend today!

			U.S.	Canadian
LCH	CS	Cassette series—includes album cover	$29.50	$37.50
		Individual cassettes—include messages		
		A and B	5.00	6.35

These prices are effective as of January 1987 and are subject to change without notice.

LCH 1-A: *Royal Mail in the Postman's Bag*
Revelation 1
   B: *Everything but the One Thing*
Revelation 2:1–7

LCH 2-A: *When Suffering Strikes*
James 1:12, Revelation 2:8–11
   B: *Ministering Where Satan Dwells*
Revelation 2:12–17

LCH 3-A: *Jezebel in the Church*
Revelation 2:18–29
   B: *A Morgue with a Steeple*
Revelation 3:1–6

LCH 4-A: *Open-Door Revival*
Revelation 3:7–13
   B: *Our Number One Spiritual Battle*
Revelation 3:14–19

LCH 5-A: *The Case of the Excluded King*
Revelation 3:20–22
   B: *Will You Lead or Lag?**
1 Corinthians 14, Exodus 18

*This message was not a part of the original series but is compatible with it.

Ordering Information

U.S. ordering information: You are welcome to use our toll-free number (for Visa and MasterCard orders only) between the hours of 8:30 A.M. and 4:00 P.M., Pacific time, Monday through Friday. The number is **(800) 772-8888.** This number may be used anywhere in the continental United States excluding California, Hawaii, and Alaska. Orders from those areas are handled through our Sales Department at **(714) 870-9161.** We are unable to accept collect calls.

Your order will be processed promptly. We ask that you allow four to six weeks for delivery by fourth-class mail. If you wish your order to be shipped first-class, please add 10 percent of the total order cost (not including California sales tax) for shipping and handling.

Canadian ordering information: Your order will be processed promptly. We ask that you allow approximately four weeks for delivery by first-class mail to the U.S./Canadian border. All orders will be shipped from our office in Fullerton, California. For our listeners in British Columbia, a 7 percent sales tax must be added to the total of all tape orders (not including first-class postage). For further information, please contact our office at **(604) 272-5811.**

Payment options: We accept personal checks, money orders, Visa, and MasterCard in payment for materials ordered. Unfortunately, we are unable to offer invoicing or COD orders. If the amount of your check or money order is less than the amount of your purchase, your check will be returned so that you may place your order again with the correct amount. All orders must be paid in full before shipment can be made.

Returned checks: There is a $10 charge for any returned check (regardless of the amount of your order) to cover processing and invoicing.

Guarantee: Our tapes are guaranteed for ninety days against faulty performance or breakage due to a defect in the tape. For best results, please be sure your tape recorder is in good operating condition and is cleaned regularly.

Mail your order to one of the following addresses:

Insight for Living
Sales Department
Post Office Box 4444
Fullerton, CA 92634

Insight for Living Ministries
Post Office Box 2510
Vancouver, BC
Canada V6B 3W7

Quantity discounts and gift certificates are available upon request.

Overseas ordering information is provided on the reverse side of the order form.

Order Form

Please send me the following cassette tapes:

The current series: ☐ LCH CS Letters to Churches ... Then and Now

Individual cassettes: ☐ LCH 1   ☐ LCH 2   ☐ LCH 3
                ☐ LCH 4   ☐ LCH 5

I am enclosing:

$ _____   To purchase the cassette series for $29.50 (in Canada $37.50*) which includes the album cover

$ _____   To purchase individual tapes at $5.00 each (in Canada $6.35*)

$ _____   Total of purchases

$ _____   If the order will be delivered in California, please add 6 percent sales tax

$ _____   U.S. residents please add 10 percent for first-class shipping and handling if desired

$ _____   *British Columbia residents please add 7 percent sales tax

$ _____   Canadian residents please add 6 percent for postage

$ _____   **Overseas residents please add appropriate postage** (See postage chart under "Overseas Ordering Information.")

$ _____   As a gift to the Insight for Living radio ministry for which a tax-deductible receipt will be issued

$ _____   **Total amount due (Please do not send cash.)**

Form of payment:

☐ Check or money order made payable to Insight for Living

☐ Credit card (Visa or MasterCard only)

If there is a balance: ☐ apply it as a donation   ☐ please refund

---

Credit card purchases:

☐ Visa   ☐ MasterCard number _____

Expiration date _____

Signature _____

We cannot process your credit card purchase without your signature.

Name _____

Address _____

_____

City _____

State/Province _____ Zip/Postal code _____

Country _____

Telephone (___) _____ Radio station ___ ___ ___ ___

Should questions arise concerning your order, we may need to contact you.

Overseas Ordering Information

If you do not live in the United States or Canada, please note the following information. This will ensure efficient processing of your request.

Estimated time of delivery: We ask that you allow approximately twelve to sixteen weeks for delivery by surface mail. If you would like your order sent airmail, the length of delivery may be reduced. All orders will be shipped from our office in Fullerton, California.

Payment options: Due to fluctuating currency rates, we can accept only personal checks made payable in U.S. funds, international money orders, Visa, and MasterCard in payment for materials ordered. If the amount of your check or money order is less than the amount of your purchase, your check will be returned so that you may place your order again with the correct amount. All orders must be paid in full before shipment can be made.

Returned checks: There is a $10 charge for any returned check (regardless of the amount of your order) to cover processing and invoicing.

Postage and handling: Please add to the amount of purchase the postage cost for the service you desire. All orders must include postage based on the chart below.

Purchase Amount		Surface Postage	Airmail Postage
From	To	Percentage of Order	Percentage of Order
$ .01	$15.00	40%	75%
15.01	75.00	25%	45%
75.01	or more	15%	40%

Guarantee: Our tapes are guaranteed for ninety days against faulty performance or breakage due to a defect in the tape. For best results, please be sure your tape recorder is in good operating condition and is cleaned regularly.

Mail your order or inquiry to the following address:

Insight for Living
Sales Department
Post Office Box 4444
Fullerton, CA 92634

Quantity discounts and gift certificates are available upon request.